WILLIAM WHITECLOUD'S
SECRETS OF NATURAL SUCCESS

FIVE STEPS TO UNLOCKING YOUR GENIUS

Animal Dreaming Publishing
www.AnimalDreamingPublishing.com

William Whitecloud's
SECRETS OF NATURAL SUCCESS
Five Steps to Unlocking Your Genius

ANIMAL DREAMING PUBLISHING
PO Box 5203 East Lismore NSW 2480
AUSTRALIA
Phone +61 2 6622 6147
www.AnimalDreamingPublishing.com
www.facebook.com/AnimalDreamingPublishing

First published in 2019
Copyright text © William Whitecloud
www.WilliamWhitecloud.com

Cover concept by Beau Ravn

ISBN 978 0 9876343 1 3

All rights reserved. No part of this publication may be reproduced in whole or in part, stored in a retrievable system, or transmitted in any form or by any means, eletronic, mechanical, photocopying, recording or otherwise, without written permission of the copyright holder or publisher.

Designed by Animal Dreaming Publishing
Printed in Australia

CONTENTS

Introduction	5
Chapter 1: The First Step of Natural Success: Understanding the Function of Consciousness	33
Chapter 2: The Second Step of Natural Success: Hearing What Your Unconscious Is Saying	47
Chapter 3: The Third Step of Natural Success: Preparing the Fertile Ground for Your Genius to Emerge	83
Chapter 4: The Fourth Step of Natural Success: Following Through	141
Chapter 5: The Fifth Step of Natural Success: Using the Emotion of the True End Result	167
About the Author	219
Other books by William	221

INTRODUCTION

The Sufis say that light doesn't travel; it unfolds out of itself. Well, this book kind of happened that way. I did not sit down to write *my* commandments for living in alignment with *Creative Spirit*. Rather, I sat down with the intention of allowing *Creative Spirit* to dictate through me *Her* instructions for engaging with *Her* for the purpose of co-creating brilliant outcomes in life, and most especially the sublime life all of us are quite capable of living. And so the content and narrative of this book flowed out of me a bit like a meandering river, to arrive finally at its destination: a comprehensive guide to living life as an expression of our highest potential. I'm sure that if you allow yourself to drift along with the flow of the following pages and let the scenery unfold, you will be delighted by the wealth of information contained in my *Secrets of Natural Success*, and by the end come to realize you have been gifted with some of the most amazing information you can ever come across concerning accessing your latent power and employing it in the creation of miracles. I say this humbly. For, though I call them my secrets, I don't mean to imply that they originate from me, only that I am the messenger dutifully organizing and delivering the message. I sincerely hope that you will come to cherish the information contained within these pages as I have and, in time, in your own way, give it away to others. We all have within us the ability to naturally succeed in creating the best life possible, and we most certainly deserve to be supported in that possibility.

Let me start off by mentioning that the word *natural* is derived from *nature* and, though we often forget it, we human beings are actually part of nature. We have evolved since the beginning of time to fit in with and thrive in the world around us. Which means we should be able to flow with life as naturally and easily as leopards and crocodiles do in their habitats. The truth is that we live in a benign universe that naturally supports us in flowing to our best life possible, a life way beyond the best we can even imagine. And we have all been endowed with the personal talents, gifts, and creative faculties—what I call our *Natural Ability*—to allow us to work in harmony with the universe, and receive life's bounty in the form of a life we truly love.

NATURAL ABILITY

I didn't appreciate it at the time but I learned a lot about *Natural Ability* and *Natural Success*—success that flows from engaging and employing our *Natural Ability*—from the African trackers I hunted and patrolled with in my youth. Back in those days the countryside was littered with wild animals. It was nothing to see herds of impala in the thousands and wildebeest herds of five hundred or more. A clearing in the bush would be covered with layers of tracks from a wide variety of animals, including antelope and predators such as hyena and leopard. One time I was out scouting the boundaries of our vast cattle ranch for signs of poaching. The tracker I was paired with stopped to take a closer look at the earth. He straightened himself again, now wearing a happy grin on his face.

"What is it?" I asked.

"This spoor here," he said, pointing with his spear at a confusion of hoof prints, "I know this one. It belongs to a very rare animal—a white wildebeest."

Intrigued, I strolled over to where the tracker stood

wearing nothing but a monkey-skin loincloth and a pair of homemade sandals fashioned from discarded Land Rover tires. I could hardly distinguish all the tracks, let alone notice any outstanding characteristics in the amorphous set of prints he poked at.

"How can you tell that it's the spoor of a white wildebeest?" I quizzed him skeptically.

"He has only one horn," the tracker replied matter-of-factly. "He walks like this." He mimed a four-legged creature listing to the side.

It wasn't unknown for the trackers to take the piss out of young greenhorns like me. An albino animal is a rare sight in the bush and if a white wildebeest did live on our property I assumed I would have either seen it or heard mention of it. Not wanting to be shown up as a gullible fool, I asked the tracker casually whether he could lead me to this distinguished animal so that I could see it for myself. "If you like," he shrugged. "When he passed by here earlier he didn't have a drink yet, so we'll find him around the dam below that mountain there."

We set out on what I calculated would be a two-mile walk. At first we crossed an open plain, and then we had to push through thick bush with no pathways offering signs of animal traffic. Blazing our way through the tangled undergrowth was hard work. Although I watched the scout closely, I never once caught him looking down at the ground for tracks. The fact that he wasn't bothering to track the wildebeest convinced me he really was pulling my leg.

Half an hour later, when we finally crashed out of the thick savanna vegetation into the well-grazed clearing that surrounded the waterhole, herds of impala and kudu and zebra trotted away from the water and then stopped to regard us curiously from the tree line on the opposite bank. There were no wildebeest in sight. The dirt around us was overlaid with thousands of tracks from every species of animal that called this part of the Great Rift Valley of Africa home.

I was curious to see how the tracker would go picking up and following any spoor here. He didn't pay attention to anything around us, though. His gaze fell on something beyond the far tree line. After a while I caught sight of what he was looking at. A journey of giraffe was nibbling delicately at the acacia treetops, moving leisurely away from us towards the nearby mountain. The scout nodded his head in satisfaction. "They are down there," he pointed his spear in the opposite direction.

To my dismay, we turned back into the thick bush behind us and headed downstream of the dam, keeping well away from the dry watercourse. After about half a mile we cut across the drainage line into more open parkland. Now, for the first time since he had showed me the alleged albino wildebeest tracks, the tracker took an interest in the ground again. When we had walked for a little while without him finding what he had evidently been looking for, he stopped and nodded confidently. "Good, they are there," he pointed back towards the dam. I peered through the widely spaced tree trunks, but I couldn't see anything other than a few impala with their heads down and tails twitching. Somewhere out of sight a zebra barked.

"I don't see anything," I said dubiously. By now I was convinced the tracker was full of shit, and I was beginning to think about what I could do to him in reprisal for trying to make a fool of me.

"They are coming this way. Let's wait for them." He sat down nonchalantly against a tree, motioning for me to do the same.

I sat cross-legged on the hard earth with my rifle cradled in my lap. As skeptical as I was, I still found myself looking eagerly for some sign of the phantom herd of wildebeest. A part of me wanted to believe that this native of the bush did indeed possess some kind of supernatural ability for tracking elusive animals. But there was also that side of me that was sure I would be disappointed. I began shifting uncomfortably as my ass cheeks turned numb. My companion, meanwhile, sat calmly with his eyes closed, his serenity adding to my irritation.

When the wildebeest finally arrived, I heard them before

Introduction

I saw them. My heart leapt at the faint sound of hooves clicking against stones in the dry riverbed. The sound grew louder. Soon I could hear the animals tugging at the winter grass and munching on the dry straw. The ground began to tremble as they clambered up the gulley walls and ambled onto the verge to our right. Before long a phalanx of the dark bovine-looking creatures was grazing its way straight towards us. Because of their poor eyesight, and the fact that the wind wasn't blowing directly towards them, they didn't notice us until they were virtually on top of us. Even then they did not shy away, only warning us with sharp snorts not to try anything funny.

I watched in amazement as wildebeest grazed contentedly all around me. There were hundreds of them. A cow walked so close to me I could have poked her in the ribs with my rifle barrel. Her calf ran up and tried to butt under her belly to get at her teats. She kicked it away, and the startled little antelope nearly staggered back into my lap. I was in such awe that by the time the last stragglers in the herd were filing past us, I had completely forgotten about the one horned albino we were supposed to find.

A soft, low-pitched whistle snapped me out of my reverie. I looked over at the tracker. He urged me with his eyes to look into the parkland before us. I didn't see it at first because my eyes were unaccustomed to the sight of anything milk-colored in the khaki savanna. All I could see were the same impala that had been there before, with distinctive black McDonald's arches emblazoned on their rumps. Then I caught a movement and suddenly the white wildebeest came into relief. He stood like some enchanted apparition, beautiful and unreal. Something about his divergent coloring, and the complete lack of camouflage it afforded, gave him a regal bearing, as if he were some princely being who could not last too long in the wide world without a protective escort. I held my breath, afraid that he would vanish at the slightest disturbance.

"He's not close enough to see his missing horn," the tracker whispered. "I'll lure him closer. Pass me your hat."

I gave him a stern look of discouragement, but he was insistent. He gesticulated assertively for me to throw him my hat. Reluctantly I took it off and threw it over to him, Frisbee-style. He caught it deftly by the rim as it passed by his face. Holding the hat with his teeth, he got on to his hands and knees and began crawling towards the wildebeest. As he advanced, he began snorting through his nose as loudly as he could.

I watched the wildebeest anxiously, expecting it to bolt at any moment. Instead, the glorious animal surveyed the tracker's approach in complete puzzlement. When its curiosity could not be contained any longer, it trotted towards him to get a closer look. Still not able to make out what the strange creature on all fours was, the pale wildebeest snorted, challenging whatever it was to make itself known, at which point the tracker stopped his advance. Now he swung my hat from side to side with his mouth and carried on snorting sharply. After a few more dissatisfied snorts of his own, the wildebeest charged closer again, then closer, and closer, until eventually he stood only a couple of car lanes' distance away from the tracker.

From that close, the albino antelope didn't look all that magnificent. He was a bit on the fragile side, being of a slighter stature than his brothers who had walked by earlier. His coat was mangy and streaked with dirt, and his missing horn gave him a rather absurd appearance. Yet there was still something endearing about him—maybe his overall vulnerability, amplified by the eternally perplexed frown on his face. Now he maintained his current distance from the tracker, uncertain of what he was dealing with. He kept on snorting and shaking his head, expecting the creature facing him to give some sign of its identity. Finally the tracker rose to his feet. "It's me, you dumb beast," he laughed.

The wildebeest pranced sideways in fright, and then, seeming to recognize the tracker, approached him tentatively, throwing its head from side to side playfully. Man and beast stood regarding each other only a car length apart.

"So, White One," the tracker said finally, "how are you

today, my friend? Still not ready to feed the hyenas and vultures, heh?" Then he shooed it away, and the gangly beast galloped off as if it was a horse just unsaddled and let loose in its favorite meadow.

You can only imagine how awed and humbled I was by that experience. And I've had many equally incredible encounters with that same man and others like him. It's extraordinary how at one those scouts are with their world, how in touch they are with it and well informed by it. They have nothing, sometimes getting about only in skins and with a stick in their hand, in an environment where the likes of you and I would perish even holding a high-powered rifle. Yet they need for nothing. The elements guide them and provide for them. All they need to thrive in their domain is awareness, to pay attention to the signs. The skies and the direction of the wind and the patterns of traffic on the ground and the animal calls and the condition of the land tell them everything—navigating them through the bush—and leading them to spectacular end results.

African guides have walked me within a few paces of wild lions, urged me to run away from elephants still a mile away, fed me wild honey they found following little birds, helped me apprehend poachers they tracked over bald granite mountains. They know at a glance if a river is safe to cross, or whether a grove of trees will make a good campsite. A sniff of the air tells them whether the rains will come or clear. Sometimes they refuse to get out of bed or work in a certain area or accompany a particular individual. To you and me their ways are seemingly capricious, and mostly mysterious. But as far as they themselves are concerned, it's just normal to be attuned to their environment, to soak up the signs and automatically compute them into obvious conclusions. Most remarkable of all is the degree to which the trackers entrust their lives to their *Natural Ability*. Every day of their life they walk through the shadow of the valley of death, and every day they reach the other side, not just alive, but with their hearts singing and their soul tanks full.

As I've implied, nature, in fact, intended that we all live

in the same way these men of the bush do. Though you and I live in a technologically advanced world, it doesn't mean that we can't be in tune with ourselves and our environment and use that connection to be guided in living remarkable lives. We can and should! We have the same powers, the same gifts, and the same *Natural Ability* as the African guides I have hung out with in the wilds. And those innate attributes will serve us equally well in modern life as they will in nature. They are far from redundant, far from obsolete. I would go so far as to say, that kind of instinctive intelligence is perhaps more relevant and necessary than ever before in our history. The capacity to be at one with our world is a function of Soul, and the consequences of a soulless existence are plain to see: struggle, alienation, environmental degradation, escalating social tensions and hostility, to name just a few.

It's obviously true that mostly we do not live in the way we were meant to live. We do not live in a way where we allow ourselves to be led by the universe to having our lives be exactly the way we would love them to be. We tend to see life as something to be fought, controlled, and dominated by the strength of our bodies and minds or, for some of us, that it is necessary to hand over our lives to other people or powers we hope will do that for us.

Shifting from this forceful, effort-filled, and oftentimes desperate way of being to a more graceful, creative approach to life is a whole artform, which I will cover in the chapters of this book. And the reward for you will be nothing short of the power to be the master of your own life. I learned this conclusively when I wrote my first book, *The Magician's Way*.

THE MAGICIAN'S WAY

I grew up with a father who was quite crazy, to put it mildly. His African nickname was "Jigga Kanda," which in SiSwati means "man whose head spins on his shoulders." Like most people, he wasn't a one-dimensional cardboard cutout. He had a very sweet and caring side to him, but he could also be harshly critical and violently demanding. He'd sack our

Introduction

cook for bringing him cold coffee, and the trackers I went hunting with in my teens used to laugh about how in the old days he would take shots at them with his rifle if they disturbed the antelope they were stalking. He controlled his world by simulating a ticking bomb that everyone else was forever doing their level best to prevent going off.

No doubt "Kanda" had many issues, not least of all was undiagnosed and untreated post-traumatic stress disorder from World War II. He didn't talk about the war much, but sometimes after a few drinks he'd try to describe what it was like advancing with General Montgomery's front line into the jaws of the German defenses in the Battle of El Alamein, or the horror of being bombed by a thousand American Flying Fortresses flying wingtip to wingtip over Monte Cassino, indiscriminately unloading their deadly payloads on enemy and allies alike. You have to feel for someone whose last conscious memory was being shaken like a cocktail inside his tin can of an armored car as all around bombs exploded and bullets whined, before waking up months later on a hospital ship in the Indian Ocean, covered in plaster from head to toe, burning up with malarial fever. My father weighed ninety-five pounds when he got back to his home port of Durban, South Africa, where, after five years of continuous combat in North Africa and Italy, he found out that his wife and two little girls were now living with another man.

I was never privy to all of what drove his misbehaviors, but it was no secret that, for all his fantastic accomplishments, Kanda's biggest demon was a gigantic sense of intellectual inferiority. He had grown up the son of a judge in a time when dyslexia was not understood, and his own authoritarian father had treated him very cruelly in relation to his learning difficulties. Consequently, Kanda never finished school and, though he went on to carve a massive sugar and citrus estate out of virgin bush in the wilds of Africa, complete with a system of mills, clinics, schools, canals, dams, roads, bridges, hundreds of staff houses, workshops, airfields, warehouses, and fruit packing plants, he could not even write a letter without my mother's help.

And for some reason—maybe because I was the unplanned child who had stopped him from emigrating abroad, where he had hoped to make a better life—he projected all that intellectual shame and frustration onto me.

My father, whom I loved so much and thought was the greatest man alive, missed no opportunity in making me feel like I was a total imbecile. Anything I didn't understand, couldn't immediately get the hang of, or didn't do in accordance with his exacting standards meant to him that I was stupid, and he did not hold back from letting me know that in the harshest of terms. Even faults that were, strictly speaking, unrelated to my intelligence reflected, in his eyes, on what an idiot I was. If I fumbled with a lock when trying to open a cattle gate or if I floundered in the swimming pool when I was learning to swim, unable to coordinate my kicking and arm strokes, it was because I was, in his words, "a thick head, a numbskull." You can imagine how much confidence this helped me develop in my own intellectual capacity!

In subsequent chapters I will demonstrate compellingly how the patterns of experience in early childhood form a template for what we attract in later life. Certainly that was the case for me. The shaming did not stop with my father. When I went to school I became the lightning rod for my teachers' ridicule. They seemed to delight in pointing out how spectacularly stupid I was. One particular math teacher used to get a big kick out of amusing the rest of my class with my pathetic test scores. He even went so far as to read out my answers with a comic timing that had the other kids in stitches. Perhaps the most embarrassing experience of all was when this same teacher found a stunted *Lord of the Flies*-inspired story I had tried to write in the middle of my exercise book and read it out to great jeers and roars of mocking laughter. Needless to say, offering up anything of myself, learning, and having my capability tested terrified me, and as a result I dropped out of school a victim of my fate—one of life's rejects, without any prospects for a consequential future.

It is not the scope of this story to take you through the

hardships I suffered as a result of my intellectual inferiority complex. Having an incomplete education made it tough enough, but most of my misery arose from my own sense of worthlessness. Fortunately for me I ultimately fell into the unstructured world of Creative Development, where "not knowing anything" is an asset (a point we'll discuss in depth later). For years I coasted along in relative obscurity teaching small groups the art of creative manifestation in the Australian countryside. That it was an art and not a science, and that I practiced my vocation anonymously, meant I was not subject to the harsh glare of critical authority figures. It was nice and safe. Nice and safe, that is, until it occurred to me that I should codify the creative principles I taught by writing a book on the subject.

Imagine the horror I felt at the idea of myself writing a metaphysical treatise. This was in the days before the popularization of quantum physics, which would ultimately give my creative theories a good measure of credence and respectability. But at the time, I was espousing scientifically heretical principles that would be, to my paranoid mind, subject to the scrutiny of a harshly judgmental world. I mean, me! Me, who had no brains, who had no literary training, who hardly ever read anything, let alone wrote so much as a letter. People had been burned at the stake for much less, I feared.

And, yet, I did have something going for me—my Creative Development training. I was able to use what I taught others to do: to tap into the *Creative Spirit* that exists beyond our rational capacities, and allow that *Natural Ability* to bring together spectacular end results—spectacular because we can never foresee the magical way in which those outcomes will come together and how much more pleasing they are than we ever expected. It was time to put my premises to the ultimate test and create the thing I believed most impossible for me to accomplish.

My intellectual insecurities were not my only problem, though. A serious complication was that I chose to write my book at the same time as I was undergoing a radical eleven-month chemotherapy treatment. Fever, nausea, chronic fatigue, blinding headaches, hallucinations, and a crushing depression that sat on my chest like an oversized gorilla were some of the two hundred symptoms I suffered on a daily basis. One of the main ingredients of the chemical cocktail I was taking was Ribavirin, which reduced my red blood cell count by between thirty and forty percent. Red blood cells carry oxygen to the rest of our cells, so imagine existing for a year in an oxygen-starved body. Climbing into bed was a task equal to ascending Mt. Everest!

In retrospect I appreciate what an insane plan that was, but in my ignorance of clinical matters, I figured I would have a lot of free time. Perhaps it was an *Unconscious* strategy to have the chemo to blame in the likely event that I failed. Whatever the case was, I sat down in my fevered, excruciating state and used my training to tap into my *Genius*. And lo and behold, out of me, or more precisely, through me, poured a book that didn't in any way resemble the one I had set out to write.

It was an outrageous process. Not just because of how sick I was or untrained in writing. I had expected to write a nonfiction self-help book covering everything I knew about my subject. Instead, from the very first page emerged a story that trashed most of the ideas I originally had for the book and introduced new ones I had never even thought of before. I was writing down words I hadn't ever used—didn't even know what they meant—but which, when I looked them up in the dictionary, expressed precisely what I wanted to say. More astonishing than anything was the unexpectedness of the narrative. In my mind, I was writing for a sensitive New Age audience, and here my characters were getting down and dirty in a topless joint. But even before that, the story starts with the main character getting a golf lesson. To me there isn't a more exasperating, painful waste of time than golf; yet the game became a profound metaphor for conveying the essence of my theme—how your focus creates your reality—and introduced a compelling language for the premises in the book. If you've read it, you know what a powerful concept the *swing circle* is.

The Magician's Way became the biggest selling metaphysical book in Australia by a local author, ever! It reached number one on Amazon—overall, and not just in some category. Hundreds of thousands of people have read it. Tens of thousands of people have used the knowledge contained in it to improve their lives, or at the very least their golf games, which for some is beyond a miracle. Marriages have been saved by it. Fortunes made. Personal tragedies averted. Most heartwarming of all, scores of teenagers have written to me to thank me for writing the book and to tell me how it saved them from committing suicide or being losers in life and put them back on track. As a result of the book's success, my profile was elevated to a level where I became the most highly sought-after Personal Development trainer and coach in the land. That book made me millions of dollars, and more than ten years later it continues to pay massive dividends. Consequently, I have been able to live the most ideal life I could hope for, indulging my passions, supporting my family in theirs, contributing meaningfully to wildlife conservation and social causes in Africa, having access to whatever and whomever I want, and creating exactly what I love.

From my experience of writing *The Magician's Way*, I now definitely know for a fact that we are all endowed with personal *Genius*—a *Natural Ability*—and that when we tap into that aspect of ourselves, success becomes a natural part of our lives. When we connect with that *Creative Spirit* within, we harmonize with the miraculous nature of existence and bring into being extraordinary creations that defy our expectations of what is possible, and simultaneously enrich ourselves and all that we are a part of.

STRAP YOURSELF IN FOR AMAZING

If you're reading this book, there's a strong likelihood that you have some sense of the shining, unlimited capacity that exists within you; that, in fact, you know there is much more to who you really are than meets the eye. I know that you yearn to express your brilliance. Maybe there are times when it has shone through in some way before, leaving you breathless at the wonder and possibility of life. Maybe it's not so rare but still a random, un-mastered experience. Or even a consistent experience, but only working for you in some areas of your life and not in others. Whatever the case may be, whatever category you fit into, the process of accessing your unlimited, infallible *Natural Ability* and making it work for you at will remains a mystery. But now you're ready to learn how to master living your life as an expression of your highest potential, so that you can easily and dependably create what you love. So, my goal in revealing to you my *Secrets of Natural Success* is to take you from your latent desire for living your greatness to where your talent and *Genius* has exploded out of you. I want to give you a thorough understanding of what it takes to live a *Genius* life and the tools to achieve it.

If I am right, and you are indeed ready for the journey, you better strap yourself in to your seat. It's going to be a wild and wonderful ride. I'm going to take the lid off what holds you back in life and show you, for real, how you can unleash the power of your creative potential. There is an observable, self-evident correlation between your level of creativity and the level of success you naturally experience in life. My aim in the following pages is to establish the relationship between creativity and success, as well as educate you in the five straightforward steps to exponentially boosting your creativity and facilitating *Natural Success* in every area of your life:

1. Understanding the function of *Consciousness*
2. Hearing what your *Unconscious* is saying
3. Preparing the fertile ground for your *Genius* to emerge
4. Following through
5. Using the emotion of the true end result

Natural Success, you will come to learn, is a journey from *Unconsciousness* to *Consciousness* (or should I say to

Super Consciousness?). If you are not familiar with this language, have no fear, its meaning will soon be clear to you, and you will quickly come to appreciate the powerful, life-changing principles these words convey.

THE FAILURE OF EDUCATION

Before any journey begins towards a known destination, it is always useful, and I'd even say essential, to know where you are starting out from. So, just briefly, let's establish our starting point: *You don't believe you have "it" in you*. None of us do. It's not personal. But unless I make it personal to you, I'm going to let you off the hook about something you have to be honest about from the get-go. Pretending otherwise will only dilute your resolve to find *"it"* again.

When I address audiences in Sydney or London or Los Angeles or other cities around the world, I always ask them to put up their hands if they genuinely believe that *Genius* resides in every single human being. Everyone puts up their hand; you can feel the conviction in the room. We instinctively know the truth. So how come, then, that virtually every one of those people who does believe hasn't demonstrated their *Genius* capacities so far? How come they haven't written genuine best-sellers, as they wish they could? How come they don't have booming businesses, as they wish they could? How come they don't have the financial security they long for? How come they don't have rocking relationships? How come they are not free to make the choices they would love to? Because, like you, they know in their hearts that *Genius* exists, but they don't believe in their minds that they have it in them. Let me say that again: they know in their hearts, but they don't believe in their minds.

The truth is that most people don't have success naturally in their lives. They are victims of circumstances. In the first decade of this century the world was gripped in the fever of a faux economic boom. Central banks, desperate to stave off a global recession threatened by the 9/11 Twin Tower terror attacks in New York City, had lowered interest rates to rock-bottom. China's insatiable demand for resources was sending commodity prices sky-high. Last but not least, a huge property price bubble had formed, thanks to low interest rates and financial institutions deciding to lend money on the basis of the increasing value of properties and not the ability of borrowers to repay their debt. Every man and his dog were making money in the stock market. Nurses and bus drivers were remodeling homes and building property portfolios. Mid-level managers were being recruited into senior executive positions.

The economic boom coincided with the proliferation of a metaphysical principle known as the *Law of Attraction*, which basically holds that persistent mental concentration on an object of desire will magnetically attract that object into your life. It seemed to work great. A lot of folks at that time put their material success down to the power of their own focus. I remember a friend of mine, Mark, a family man with four children, whose self-managed pension portfolio had multiplied four hundred percent in eighteen months, telling me in a smug voice, "It's the *Law of Attraction*, William." Memories are short, people have already forgotten, but there was a brief time when everyone thought their fleeting good fortune was a function of their own magical powers. Mark closed down a good business he owned, worth at least half a million dollars, without even bothering to try to find a buyer for it. After all, why bother with a trifling amount like five hundred thousand dollars when you've found the pot of gold at the end of the rainbow?

There were a lot of swollen heads and puffed-out chests in 2007. That is, before the infamous Global Financial Crisis struck and the economy went backwards—fast! The stock market crashed, the resources boom busted, and the property bubble burst. More people than not were over-extended and had to liquidate their properties and stocks at a loss. Everywhere workers and top executives were losing their jobs. All those temporary hotshots soon found themselves begging for any paying work they could get, with all areas of their lives in disarray.

And therein was the hard lesson their bruised—and in

some cases battered—*Egos* had to learn: that their good fortune had been created by forces other than their persistent mental concentration, and that those same external forces had dashed their fortunes. What circumstances giveth, circumstances taketh away. In the second week of the stock market collapse, my friend Mark, whose pension portfolio had made him a millionaire for a brief time, called me in tears, "The *Law of Attraction* isn't working anymore, William." I really felt bad for him. By virtue of his own naivety, he and his family were in for some rough years. But there it was: in Mark's mind, the *Law of Attraction* had the power, not him. Which goes to my point. None of us believe that the power is in us.

Historically this wasn't always the case. In ancient Rome, the *Genius* was the guiding spirit of a person. In Latin, as a verb, it means "to bring into being, create, produce." Because the achievements of remarkable individuals seemed to indicate the presence of a particularly powerful *Genius*, the word took on the connotation of prodigious inspiration or talent. *Education* is derived from the Latin word *educere*, meaning "to draw out or bring forth."

From an understanding of *Genius* and the true meaning of *education*, we realize that the power, the knowledge, is in us, and there needs to be a process by which we learn to draw on that inner wisdom and creativity as our guiding principle in life. But our so-called education system does the exact opposite of that. It serves the function of ramming prescribed knowledge down our throats. And, by the way, I don't just blame schools for the problem. At every level of society, including in our homes and in the workplace, we are conditioned to believe that the power is outside of us, that we have to learn from, emulate, and copy others. Most insidiously, by a long-term, stealthy process, we wind up assuming that there are rules that govern every aspect of life and that the one who can best learn the rules and best apply them will cope best in life.

When I think of this subject, my daughter, India, always comes tearfully to mind. She has the most beautiful hand-writing. And that's not the opinion of a biased father, either. I've heard many people admire her neat, aesthetic style, even before they knew that she was the author. How she does it I don't know, because she holds the pen in the most contorted way imaginable. No one could replicate her grip if they tried, let alone write anything intelligible using it. But, hey, it works for her, and you'd think that's all that counts. It's perplexing, then, that every single teacher she had in elementary school, through a series of conventional public and supposedly enlightened private schools, beat on India for the way she held her pen. I mean, they got seriously worked up about it. Sometimes the poor little thing actually lost marks for her assignments or tests, not for the quality of her work but for the peculiar method she used to write with. One teacher even assigned someone to sit next to India with instructions to hit her hand with a ruler every time she lapsed into her offensive writing style. What she was learning from these alleged "educators" was that the process is more important than the end result, and that her way of doing things is wrong—and bad!

At the other end of the educational spectrum, a young acquaintance of mine, Josh, began a Master of Business Administration (MBA) course some years ago. At a dinner party held by a mutual friend, Josh regaled the rest of us with the bizarre story of his first meeting with his Marketing lecturer. Apparently this man, affecting a rumpled professorial demeanor, walked into the classroom, dropped a pile of books on his desk with a massive thud, and without even introducing himself, waved an accusing finger at the startled students before him, many of whom were older than himself, and growled menacingly, "Don't any of you think that you're fucking Steve Jobs."

Everyone knew what he meant by that because he proceeded to make his meaning clear. He was putting them on notice that Steve Jobs, the genius behind the success of Apple, was a freak of nature. They weren't like him. They shouldn't think that they were capable of the inspiration that could independently dream up insanely appealing products that their customers would love and give their teeth for. The MBA students shouldn't kid themselves that they had that kind of genius in them. And lucky for them, the lecturer was going to train them in reliable methods of market research, which would help them find out from the market what it wanted or needed, so that the business grads could make money for themselves and their bosses by catering to the demands of their customers.

At school and college, and just about everywhere else, you get taught that you don't have it in you. Moreover, you get taught that there is a right way to do things, and you get taught what others believe *the way* is. There are some basic misconceptions that we tend to be ruled by. And they have a lot to answer for. Because it doesn't matter what else you get right in life, these misconceptions will always hold you back. It's like swimming against a tide. Even if you know how to swim, it doesn't help if you're swimming headlong into the current. You won't get far, and if you keep it up, sooner or later you're going to get exhausted and start drowning. Therefore, as we go along, I'm going to be disabusing you of some creatively fatal misconceptions—notions and beliefs that have you operating and manifesting at a very low level creatively rather than at the high-level creative capacity you are so capable of. For now, though, we're addressing the most fundamental misconception of all: that you don't know for yourself, and that you must find out from someone else who does know.

Be a finder not a seeker, I always say. Except most people have it the other way around, much to their own creative detriment. Nowadays everyone is desperately searching for the formula to everything. Catering to this epidemic, there are workshops covering literally every aspect of life—how to be a man, how to be less of a man, how to be a woman, how to have sex, how to find love, how to heal, how to make money, how to find peace. I mean, you name it and there's a course on how you do that thing right. And here's the problem: when you don't believe you know for yourself, you fall back on others for *the way*, for the formula.

The limitations of formulas for being and doing should be self-evident. Not that she would want to, as far as I'm aware, but how could Elizabeth Gilbert, author of the mega-best-selling *Eat, Pray, Love*, ever give you the formula to writing a best-seller? You are not a clone of her. You have a unique imagination, vision, and voice that cannot ever express itself in the same way as Ms. Gilbert. It's daft to think that individual brilliance is transferable. But not only that, the real sin of relying on someone else's formula is that it stunts your creativity. Worse than the fact that it will limit you to the known quantity of anything (i.e., to what's been done in the past), worse than the fact that it can never be exactly relevant to your current situation or tailored to your own style of being and doing, worse than all the many limitations I could point out—when you rely on formulas, you're telling yourself that you don't have it in you. And that is the most damning thing that can ever happen to you.

Behavioral scientists are well aware of what I'm talking about. They call it "the Matthew effect," after a passage in the Bible that states, "To those who have, more shall be given, and to those who have not, even the little they have shall be taken away from them." When you fail to step up and create for yourself, when you rely on someone else's *Genius* to guide you in life, you're assuming that you haven't got what they've got—you're behaving like a *Have Not*. So, you don't have to take my word for it; even scientists will tell you that the bottom-line determinant for success in life is a person's own sense of wholeness, an ultimate reliance on their own inner substance. As Norman Seeff, the brilliant photographer and creative mentor to corporate geniuses like Steve Jobs, said, *Genius* is an inside job.

You'll really get what I'm saying as we dive in deeper. For now, just consider this: For many years a significant spiritual publishing house ran a competition called *The Next Top Spiritual Author*. Every year tens of thousands of hopeful authors entered the competition. Every year hundreds of thousands—or maybe millions—of people voted on it. You'd think that the person picked as the best out of thirty thousand or more writers would be pretty amazing, that they'd written a stellar book. I've asked thousands of audience members at my workshops and talks if they can name a winner of this contest or a book written by one of its winners. But no one has ever heard of them. I met a woman who told me she was a finalist in that competition, and she confessed that, now years later, she had not even published her manuscript yet. How could it be that a person judged in the top six out of tens of thousands of writers hadn't sold a single book?

My question is, why aren't the winners of *The Next Top Spiritual Author* contest among the names that come to mind when you think of spiritual authors? And the answer is, because none of them have created their offering relying on their *Genius*, in the way that the authors you have heard of and love did. What separates Paulo Coelho and Marianne Williamson and Neale Donald Walsch and Eckhart Tolle from the wanna-be gurus is *Genius*. They write brilliant books, works that are diamonds amongst the mountains of sand and pebbles.

You see, the formula that is typically offered for book success is marketing, not writing, because those offering the formulas don't believe in the *Genius* of their writing clients. I won't bore you with the marketing formulas. They are well known in the industry and they sound really solid, like if you just follow them faithfully you're bound to be the next Deepak Chopra. But they don't work. For the hundreds of thousands of people giving the formulas their best shot, the list of household names never grows by more than a couple every year—which is astounding, if you really think about it.

But if you were a spiritual author, can you imagine how astronomically valuable it would be for you to be able to connect with the *Genius* that writes a book that elevates you stratospherically above the hundreds of thousands of aspiring authors in your field? Rather than paying a fortune for some tired formula that makes you an unremarkable also-ran? Now we're talking about a genuine game-changer, a true paradigm shift. Not just in relation to writing, of course, but in every aspect of your life or field of endeavor.

So, are you ready to claim back your inner substance? To reconnect with your own *Genius*? To live your life as a *Have*? If the answer is *YES*, this book is for you. And don't worry, I won't be giving you a formula for how to do anything. What I'm going to give you are the keys to unlocking your own creativity, which will lead you to being naturally more successful at whatever you choose to create in life.

SUCCESS IS STRUCTURAL, NOT PERSONAL

When the white man was advancing across the North American continent in the eighteenth and nineteenth centuries, his rapacious land grab was brought to a dead halt along the frontiers of Texas, Oklahoma, and Kansas by a fierce tribe of Native Americans known as the Comanche. Their warriors visited such hell on the European settlers and punished the American army so badly in battle that it was thought their number was in the millions; defeating them was considered by most an impossible task, even though the number of settlers backing up on the frontier was in the millions, too. Before he was killed in the Battle of the Little Bighorn, Colonel George Custer was one of many U.S. commanders to clash with the ferocious Comanche braves, whose women, it might be noted, fought as valiantly and ruthlessly by their sides.

Astonishingly, the actual number of Comanche was closer to only twenty-five thousand men, women, and children, and their advantage lay entirely in the geography of the territory they ruled, a harsh expanse of desert covering large swathes of Northern Mexico, Arizona, New Mexico, Texas, and the lands reaching right up to present-day Colorado. You have to appreciate that back in the seventeen and eighteen hundreds, the only way of getting around was on foot or on horseback. Because the Comanche were familiar with the system of springs and waterholes across the vast desert wilderness, they could come and go as they pleased and easily evade the American troops, who didn't have the knowledge or resources necessary to survive in the God-forsaken world of Comancheria.

Finally, though, a general by the name of MacKenzie developed intelligence about the desert lands in which the Comanche ranged and got a true picture of their size and strength. Knowing where they were camped and in what numbers, and with access to a relay of water wells, MacKenzie's troops were able to penetrate Comancheria and systematically rout the disparate clans, who were once thought to be a huge, united army.

The demise of the Comanche is one of the saddest chapters in the history of the colonization of North America, which included the decimation of the bison herds of the Great Plains in a calculated bid to deny the natives their primary source of food. Yet, if considered objectively rather than sentimentally or moralistically, this story is a perfect illustration of what I mean when I say that success is structural and not personal. The Europeans piling up on the frontier were not, in fact, the inferior force that they assumed themselves to be for over a hundred years. They just didn't know their way around the desert like their indigenous foe, which meant they couldn't figure out the scope of the fight they were in or take it to the enemy. But once the American army had a map of Comancheria, and better intelligence on their adversaries, the tables were quickly turned. It took only a few years for the previously invincible "Indian" empire to be overwhelmed.

By the same token, you shouldn't assume that where you are in life means anything about your power. Just because you might be stuck or struggling in some area of your life, or not getting ahead as well as you'd like, is not a reflection of your potential. It's not personal. It's structural. It just means that you haven't got the big picture, the right perspective. But when you do get it—when the light bulb goes on—the tables will be turned. You'll naturally and automatically achieve success in any area of your life that you turn your attention to. Because the truth is, you are an awesome force of nature. You're a *Genius*.

You may not have a sense of your own *Genius* right now. But don't let your circumstances fool you. When you've got a bad cold, you might feel miserable, but you most probably don't assume that it means you're incapable of long-term health and fitness. Likewise, if you're suffering the symptoms of low-level creativity, you shouldn't assume that's the limit of your potential. If you're doing a job you hate, or if you'd rather be doing something else but can't, for the time being, see how that's possible—or if you're always getting told you're talented at something you love but you can't make a living doing it—or if you haven't ever got the time or money to do the things you'd love to do—or if you're in business and you're struggling to keep up with the competition—or if you're affected by outside conditions like the state of the economy or the job market or the outcome of an election—or if you're trying harder but not getting any further—or you're always worrying about the future—it doesn't mean anything other than you are not switched on to your *Natural Ability*, the part of you that can effortlessly rise above those circumstances.

Don't think you're alone in that. Before I got into Creative Development I had no sense of my own creative power. As a high school dropout with a history of chronic health problems, failed relationships, and woeful financial predicaments, I just assumed that I was a defective mechanical organism. I had no inkling that there was a magical ability within me that I could rely on for support in living the life of my dreams. Thanks to the failure of education, you're likely oblivious to the deeper reserves of creative power untapped inside you.

LEVELS OF CREATIVITY

Just in case you're getting the wrong idea, or have started out with some misconceptions, perhaps, let me say quickly that *Natural Success* and the creativity that engenders it have nothing to do with being artsy, or developing your IQ—and it certainly hasn't got anything to do with mystic hooey, or therapy, or having to be a certain way in life. This has everything to do with opening a doorway to a whole new way of seeing things; it's about making connections between things that have never been made before, opening up to inspirations and possibilities that your rational mind can't conceive of.

When you look at academic *Levels of Creativity* they are usually delineated something like this:

1. Unskilled Imitation
2. Skilled Imitation
3. Low-Level Derivative
4. High-Level Derivative
5. Innovative/Inventive
6. Genius

As you can see, the ascending progression of creativity starts out with an orientation that is heavily externally referenced, becoming less and less so, until it peaks at *Genius*, which is an orientation not at all influenced by what has come before. True creativity has been said to be the ability to manifest *Some Thing* from *No Thing*. In his epic Sufi poem, *The Conference of the Birds*, which is laced with creative references, Farid ud-Din Attar suggested that "if someone asks you how to do something, tell them to forget whatever they did before." He may have added, "and tell them to ignore what anyone else did before, too".

Consideration of the different degrees of musicianship might put these creative levels in perspective: kids in a garage band learning to play songs by their favorite bands obviously represent *Unskilled Imitation*; the solo artist or band members playing other artists' hits in bars and clubs have graduated to *Skilled Imitation*; tribute bands who interpret someone else's songs and perform them with a high degree of proficiency might be said to be *Low-Level Derivative*; then, at the next level, we encounter *High-Level Derivative*, the accomplished artist who does their own thing brilliantly but whose influences can still clearly be heard in what they do; and then finally the levels of *Inventiveness* and *Genius*, where the artist is in a league of their own, thrilling us with the beauty and originality of their work.

It's easy to observe the *Levels of Creativity* in the art scene or in the business world, as well, and in fact you can use it as a standard of measurement for any endeavor in life. It's also very evident that the higher levels of creativity are appreciated and valued more by society, and the rewards are exponentially greater, too. Still using the example of musicians, it's a given that kids in a garage band are going to earn nothing more than complaints from their neighbors, and that while the derivative musician might make a living, they definitely won't be making the fortunes that the geniuses like Michael Jackson and Prince and Madonna have made. People often rail against the fact that there is such a high income disparity between workers and bosses, or unknown artists and famous artists, but when you understand the intrinsic value of high-level creativity, like it or not, the discrepancy will always be so. The ability to go out there and steal fire from the Gods on behalf of humanity will always be more astronomically rewarded, because it is both an existential and a spiritual imperative. Remember this, both the parrot and William Shakespeare might learn English words, but one lives in ignominious anonymity and the other is immortalized through all time.

An important point to restate here is the one I made right at the beginning, when I told you my story about writing *The Magician's Way*: When you tap into your *Genius*, success becomes a natural part of your life. At the levels of *Imitation* and *Derivative*, you trudge mundane pathways—fulfilling ordinary tasks or offering common services within the pre-established, pre-existing order of things, your worth always depending on how much better than the next person you fit in with and serve that order. A glaring example of this sad reality is the effect globalization has had on the working and professional classes in first-world countries: millions and millions of jobs lost and ever shrinking wages and job security. Mark Cuban, the outspoken tech billionaire, is very vocal in predicting that technology, especially artificial intelligence, is not far off from making all task-oriented work redundant, including high-skilled professions such as accounting and law.

Introduction

At the level of *Genius*, though, you break out of the routine world—you become a sovereign, disruptive force, making connections between things that have never been made before, expanding the human horizon in fields as diverse as entertainment and transportation, or well-being and communications. The level of inspiration you rise to, and the high resonance of what you give out, creates an appreciative response from your world that deliberately wants to elevate you to a position where you can supply more of that marvelous juice. And, of course, the level of self-satisfaction increases commensurately, too. To see a *Genius* at work is to observe someone in his or her bliss.

Another very important point that can't be stated too often is: You have the potential to rise to the level of *Genius*. The level of creativity you currently operate from is not inherently fixed or permanent. Given the benefit of a true education, you can learn to tap into your *Natural Ability* and apply it in creating brilliant end results in every area of your life. You will be both delighted and surprised to realize what extraordinary gifts lie dormant within you. Although, you do also need to be prepared for another surprise: the likelihood that your *Genius* is not what you expect it to be. Living as an expression of your highest potential is going to be determined not only by your willingness to discover your personal creative nature, but even more by your willingness to accept and apply it. All forms of *Genius*, if expressed without reservation, lead equally to all manifestations and benefits of success. Consider this list of *Geniuses*, and how their diverse talents led them all to enormous prominence, influence, and wealth. Yes, all of them, even the saints!

Artistic Genius—Andy Warhol
Writing Genius—J.K. Rowling
Inventive Genius—Thomas Edison
Strategic Genius—Steve Jobs
Visionary Genius—Richard Branson
Empathetic Genius—Mother Teresa
Theoretical Genius—Albert Einstein

Social Genius—Nelson Mandela
Intuitive Genius—Mark Twain
Media Genius—Oprah Winfrey

Your *Genius* may or may not fit into one of these categories. There are, no doubt, as many forms of *Genius* as there are stars in the sky. As the well-known quote, dubiously attributed to Einstein, states: "Everybody is a genius. But if you judge a fish by its ability to climb a tree, it will live its whole life believing that it is stupid." What is certain is that a living, working relationship with your own *Genius* will lead to you living a richly rewarding life that will massively benefit you and all that you are a part of. The following five chapters of this book present the five straightforward steps you can take to elevating yourself to a genius level of creative ability. Learning and applying these secrets of *Natural Success* will be by far the most empowering thing you ever do in your life.

CHAPTER ONE
THE FIRST STEP OF NATURAL SUCCESS

UNDERSTANDING THE FUNCTION OF CONSCIOUSNESS

How did *success* become such a dirty word? These days it's associated with mindless greed. It's synonymous with lack of integrity, as if it's for the type of person who has no qualms profiting at the expense of others. Or that it's pursued by spiritually bankrupt individuals who burn themselves out grasping and clawing for social status and power—that it applies to those who Bob Dylan admonishes in his folk opus "Idiot Wind": "You'll find out when you reach the top / You're on the bottom." Well, that may well be the dark side of success, but to me success is achieving the power to be who we are and have our lives be the way we'd love them to be. Sadly, it's true that most people have gone to sleep to their own power.

WAKING UP

Some years ago I participated in an ayahuasca ceremony deep in the rainforests of northern New South Wales, a very picturesque part of Australia. In case you don't know, ayahuasca is a psychotropic substance extracted from a South American jungle vine, which facilitates profoundly cosmic levels of consciousness, to say the least. As is my habit, I had arrived very early, and while I waited for the ceremony to begin, I was quite startled to watch all the other participants arriving in a convoy of battered old kombi vans, each of them looking like miniature Ents, those giant tree people from Tolkien's *Lord of the Rings*. I was surrounded by the holdouts of what had been Australia's Feral Movement, a colorful tribe of nature lovers who had opted out of our materialistically driven society.

The really interesting thing, though, was that when we were given the opportunity to express our intentions for the ceremony, all these folks began praying for more abundance in their lives. They were pleading with the Spirit of Nature to grant them the resources to be able to have the things they'd love to have and create the things they'd love to create. I got to know one of the men, Terry, very well after that, and over time he divulged his dreams to me. He wanted to be an actor, and live in a beautifully designed eco house, and get down to the beach in a reliable vehicle, and go on holidays to tropical locations, and be able to provide a good life for his kids—and to have these things in a way that he could remain congruent with his social and environmental values. That was his dream, for his life to be like that. This is my definition of success—when any part of your life matches any one of your dreams.

Not that Terry knew he had any dreams. These were just things that were in his vague "would be nice" basket. If you had asked Terry what he wanted, he would have told you, "Nothing." That's a standard human response; people won't let themselves admit what they want when they can't see how they can get it. It's too painful. If we don't believe the power is in us, we assume that there are conditions that make it impossible for us to have what we love. Then we get confused about our goal and, instead of going for what we actually want, we get sidetracked into trying to remove those "negative" conditions.

In Terry's case, he had a severe mistrust of authority, which he viewed as corrupt, as did many of his Feral friends, and his way of coping with the danger he perceived in the world was to withdraw from it, as well as to look down on those who continued to participate in it. So as long as the condition of a corrupted world existed in his mind, Terry couldn't have what he wanted, which, to me, is a very disempowered position. When you start assuming that the power is in you, the outside conditions cease to have the power over what you can create in your life. You are free to be true to yourself *and* have what you love.

Sometimes powerlessness is not that easy to spot. Back in the day when I used to do some creative consulting in the corporate arena, an associate director from one of Australia's Big Four banks ended up tagging along to my public talks. He loved hanging around after and listening to my team and close associates talk about their experiences with creating. We enjoyed his company just as much. He had a smooth, urbane air about him, like a cultivated character Kevin Spacey would play in a movie. One night my operations manager looked him straight in the eye and said flatly, "So, Graham, when are you going to sign up for our training?"

We had always put Graham on a pedestal and thought of him as the most powerful and capable among us, a big-time success who made what we were creating in our lives look like child's play. Yet his answer was quite pathetic: "I really love and admire the freedom you guys have to go for whatever you want," he sighed wistfully. "I've always dreamed of playing the piano full time. But I have a wife and three children to support." It's a cliché I've heard repeated many times in one form or another.

Now, I don't know if Graham could have supported himself as a musician. Nevertheless, it was astonishing to hear a man who I had assumed, by virtue of his high station in life, was a powerful individual, profess that he had no choice other than to spend the vast majority of his life doing something that was not in line with his own true nature. It almost defines self-hatred, and most certainly characterizes the antithesis of personal power and true success: the ability to have life be the way you'd love it to be. In spite of outer appearances, Graham did not believe that the power was in him. Every night he attended my talks, he watched his supposed social inferiors sign up to live the lives they were born to live. But he couldn't. Like Terry, he was a slave to the only way he knew how to survive.

I can relate to Terry and Graham. At the time I knew them they were asleep to the *Genius* within themselves and the magnificent lives they were capable of creating. But I'm no one to judge. I was like them once—sleepwalking through life. I never considered that I was more than a mechanical carcass with some grey matter between my ears to help me navigate my circumstances as comfortably as possible—or, if I have to be honest, as painlessly as possible. I had no sense of any animating principle within me. I just thought the best I could do in life was figure out the rules as best I could and follow them to the best of my ability. I was doing a pretty good impersonation of a sheep right up until my late twenties.

Being a good sheep was tough going, though. I felt very uncomfortable in my own skin, always painfully self-conscious that I wasn't cutting it at anything I was trying to conform to. Drinking and rugby, getting worked up about politics, picking up girls, gossip, idle conversation, keeping up with the latest trends, being a diligent worker, saving for a house—whatever it was, I was ill-suited to it, like a fish out of water.

Mercifully, something terrible happened to put an end to the pretense that I was born to work 9 to 5 doing whatever society deemed as "the thing to be in"—or any of the other bullshit. I became extremely unwell. Over a ten-year period, I slid deeper and deeper into the grip of a mysterious illness. To this day nobody has ever matched my condition with a known clinical pathology. Symptomatically, it was as if aliens had visited me in my sleep and sucked my own substance out of me, leaving only the shell of my outer body. All of me was gone. I lost my mind. I couldn't remember anything, sometimes not even my own name. I was hallucinating every waking moment of my life, and many days I had tension headaches so bad that it felt as though some demonic force was using a wire garrote to slice through my skull and strangle my brain. If you can imagine suffering from a permanent hangover, that's how I felt: no energy, bilious, crummy, fevered. Blisters and scabs covered my body as I wilted into a listless and emaciated version of my former self.

It was a living nightmare. I was occupying some halfway world between life and afterlife. I had a foot in both worlds but I was in touch with neither. The most painful aspect of my condition was the sense of alienation I felt. No one could relate to what was happening to me; no one could tell me what was wrong with me. Though the medical establishment ran every test in the book and turned me inside out, there was no diagnosis, and thereby no prescription, no treatment. The best anyone could think of was to suggest that I pull myself together and, when I wasn't able to do that, right at the end, give me some deathbed counseling.

At that point of my life (or should I say death?) the only thing I had energy for was alarm. I became a concentrated ball of fearfulness. In my waking nightmare I was a piece of human garbage being shipped out of town in a refuse truck, my feeble cries for help unanswered by the living, functioning members of society, who wanted no part in any mess, human or otherwise. But then, eventually, my resistance to being ejected from this world gave way to resignation. Hanging on in abject desperation became too painful. The white-haired lady sitting at the foot of my bed was starting to make sense with her talk of my letting go and heading towards the light. After her final visit, I shuffled out of my apartment and into a park across the road to consider her morbid counsel.

I sat down forlornly on a park bench and began savoring

all the bittersweet manifestations of life around me. Mothers pushed strollers by in animated pairs, doing their circuit of the paved pathway circling the oak-lined oval. Kids were playing a game of soccer out on the emerald field, their laughter startling the seagulls swarming above like pieces of paper blowing haphazardly in the wind. An amphitheater of brownstone apartment buildings closed around the park, concentrating the sky above into a dazzling circle of blue.

An obscenely fit young man sat down next to me. His robust appearance only made me more depressed. Ignoring my body language, which strongly urged him to leave me alone, he introduced himself with a cheerful grin. His name was Greg. He steamrolled me into a conversation, and inevitably we were soon talking about what was wrong with me. As I divulged more and more about my condition, Greg surprised me by becoming increasingly fascinated by what I told him. And then he totally floored me by claiming that he not only knew exactly what was wrong with me, but that he had suffered from the very same condition. At first I was skeptical, but the more he told me about his own experience, the more convinced I became that his claim was true. He described the affliction to a T, including the physical, emotional, and psychological symptoms, and the slow perplexing slide from being mildly unwell to ending up an absolute wreck.

Oh my god, what a sweet relief to finally meet someone who understood what I was going through! And who could validate my condition as a legitimate ailment. As if meeting someone who could relate to me wasn't amazing enough, he went on to promise me that he had cured himself and that he could give me the prescription to instantly bounce back to normal health.

Imagine, though, how my hopes were dashed the moment he gave me the prescription. The cure, he told me, was eating red meat, drinking white wine with dinner, and smoking two cigarettes and drinking one or two coffees every day. That was a horrifying concept. The full weight of both the medical and alternative health establishments had me fully enrolled in avoiding all toxic substances, most especially the ingredients Greg was proposing. By then I was living on boiled cabbage, purified water, and a vast array of vitamins and Chinese herbs.

Nevertheless, a single word began forming spontaneously deep in my bowels and gurgled up through my body uninhibited by my self-conscious resistance, until it exploded joyfully in my mind. *YES!* After all, what did I have to lose? If I was going to go, I might as well go enjoying a few last indulgences. I went straight from my meeting with Greg to the closest restaurant, which was finishing up their lunch service, and ordered a steak without sides, a glass of chardonnay, a coffee, and a packet of cigarettes. This was still in the days when you could smoke in restaurants, and looking back I realize I must have been quite a sight for the other diners—an emaciated, scabby man in grubby sweatpants and a T-shirt, eating and drinking and smoking as voraciously as a starved animal.

Amazingly, and contrary to my honest expectations, Greg's prescription worked. I bounced back to good health immediately. Sure, it took a few months to regain my former weight and for all the sores on my body to heal, but I came back to life almost instantly. My energy and wits were restored in days. I stopped hallucinating and the headaches went away. I was back in the world of the living, a walking miracle. Lazarus had nothing on me. It was such an incredible turnaround that the only way people who knew me could process it was by assuming that I had just been shirking the last ten years—that, in fact, there had never been anything wrong with me in the first place. But it had happened to me, and I knew that I'd been to hell and back. And I knew how unbelievably fortunate I was to have been snatched back from the jaws of death.

Here's the thing, though. This phenomenal experience had a huge effect on me and gave me pause for a lot of deep reflection. But I didn't come away believing that there was any efficacy in Greg's prescription. I never bought the theory that there were any properties in the meat and wine and caffeine and nicotine that had cured me. Something else dawned on me. The proverbial light went on in my mind. It occurred to me that the power was in *me*! There must be something about my focus that determined my experience in life. For a whole decade I had been obsessed with being sick, and running around ever more desperately trying to find the expert who could fix me, and all that happened was I kept sliding towards my deathbed, until eventually I was lying on it. And when I abandoned the effort to stop that slide, I was instantly restored to good health. That's the connection I made—my eyes had been opened—and I became intensely curious as to how this mysterious principle worked. I wanted to learn how my focus created my reality, so that I could create my heaven on earth, rather than the hell I had been through for ten long, dreadful years.

Intention is a very powerful force. Very quickly I attracted the teachings and teachers that could help me understand my new insight. Learning and applying what I learned woke me up to who I really am and what I'm positively capable of. I have spent the last twenty-five years learning and refining everything I learned about how our focus creates our reality, and I hope that you are ready to receive the benefit of my research in a neat, coherent, and convenient package, which will allow you to awaken and engage a side of yourself that transcends all limitation and *Super Consciously* manifests a miraculous life. The place to start is understanding how consciousness works.

THE PREMISE OF PREMISES

Before we go any further, I have to clear something else up. What I am about to present you with is most definitely not a belief system. I do not subscribe to fixed ideas or immutable laws, and no creator should ever do so, as it only establishes the very limitations that *Genius* is free of. While the rational mind seeks an absolute understanding of how things are and how things work, there is no one right way. Physicists have observed the same atomic particle in two different places at the same time. If matter can bi-locate, then I put it to you that anything is possible, and we should keep an open mind about everything.

I prefer to use premises, the same way scientists do. A premise is a working assumption about the way in which something works. By using premises, you get results. If you get good results, you have a good premise. The premise doesn't even have to be true, or correspond with current scientific theory, which is constantly evolving anyway. In my lifetime I've known many competitive swimmers, starting with my older brother, George, who was on the school swimming team. Many of them were champions, and over many decades and in places as far apart as Africa and Australia, they all shared with me a very interesting technique they used for swimming faster. Their coaches taught them to imagine that their hands were paddles when they raced. When they imagined that their hands were paddles, their times were faster. Were their hands actually paddles? Obviously not. But is it a good premise for a swimmer to use? Most definitely.

From here on in, I'm going to lay out for you the most powerful creative premises I've ever come across—my *Secrets of Natural Success*—and it's up to you to try them on for size. When you do, you'll be amazed at the shifts that begin occurring in your life. Unlike the paddle premise, which increases the swimmer's speed fractionally, these premises will enhance your life experience exponentially. I must warn you, though, you ought to keep a stock of fresh underwear handy because your ride is about to get seriously turbo-charged.

ASPECTS OF CONSCIOUSNESS

As we've already seen, your level of creativity naturally determines your chances of success. Further to that, I'm proposing that your level of consciousness determines your level of creativity. By *consciousness* I mean the aspects of you that have awareness and determination, and that make up your most individual and essential nature, whether physical or metaphysical.

As a premise, the part of you that creates your reality, both in terms of perception and actual experience, is your *Subconscious*, the feminine, creative aspect of mind. The *Subconscious* is constantly receiving messages. It says "Yes" to whatever message it gets, and then draws that message into reality. The *Subconscious* does not discriminate, discern, distinguish, or make moral and ethical judgments. No matter what the message is, it just says "Yes" to it and creates accordingly.

The analogy of a womb is very appropriate. The womb, also an aspect of feminine gender, is purely fertile. Its eggs do not pick and choose the sperm that fertilizes them. The eggs have no genetic or racial biases. Whatever sperm makes it into the fallopian tube is going to seed the awaiting egg, creating through that union a new lifeform that will grow in the womb and then, when fully formed, be born into the world. So, too, with the *Subconscious*; whatever message it is seeded with gets born into reality.

Still as a premise, we are assuming that there are three different aspects of consciousness that give the *Subconscious* messages: the *Unconscious*, the *Self Conscious*, and the *Super Conscious*. The *Unconscious*, in our language, is the limiting belief system that we hold just beneath our waking self-awareness, which we have acquired through the sum of our experiences. It is not, as you will see shortly, what we call the *Ego*, but the *Ego* is driven by its content. Something else I should point out is that our *Unconscious* should not be confused with the Jungian idea of the collective unconscious, which corresponds more to our *Super Conscious*. Sometimes Jungian scholars get quite hot under the collar when they hear the *Unconscious* being associated with *Egoic* qualities, but it's just semantics. At the end of the day our premises are very similar in concept, differing only in our language.

The *Self Conscious* is the waking, self-aware part of us that is the interface between the different aspects of consciousness and existence. It's the part of us that can notice, think, analyze, decide, and choose. In this context, it shouldn't be confused with the insecure over-preoccupation with self that the term often describes.

The *Super Conscious* is our *Genius*, our intuition, higher self, soul, or God within. Some would say that it is our imagination, which it might be, but I prefer to think of the imagination as the bridge between the *Super Conscious* and the *Self Conscious*. Certainly you could say it's our *Creative Spirit*, the part of us connected to everything through all time and space, which extends beyond what we know from experience and guides us in the expression of our true nature and purpose.

These three aspects of consciousness are constantly feeding messages into your *Subconscious*, which says "Yes" and, like a good genie, manifests that command as your wish, whether you like it or not. You might not know it, you might not even like it, but you are a creating machine. You are constantly churning out reality by turning messages into experiences.

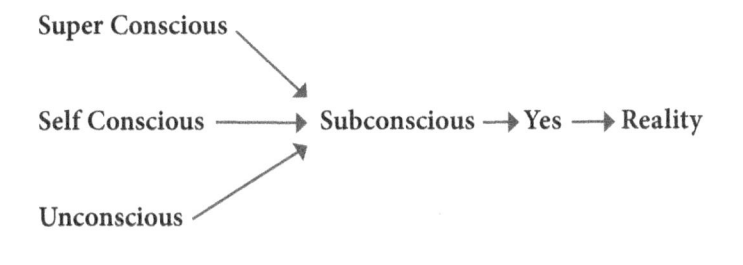

Aspects of Consciousness

Super Conscious ↘
Self Conscious ⟶ Subconscious → Yes ⟶ Reality
Unconscious ↗

In the case of my illness, which I described earlier, very obviously my *Subconscious* was being informed by my *Unconscious*, and that is the experience I created—ten years of hell that reflected my beliefs about being unviable in life.

In the case of writing *The Magician's Way*, on the other hand, very obviously my *Subconscious* was being directed by my *Super Conscious*. The result there was a best-selling book that set me up for life.

THE UNBENDABLE ARM

Now hopefully you can see what I mean by *Levels of Consciousness*, and how your level of consciousness determines your experience of life. If you would like a physical demonstration of this principle at work, there's a simple exercise you can try with another person. It's a martial arts technique we call *The Unbendable Arm*. How it works is, you take your demonstration partner's left arm and position it in a V, so that their forearm is at a ninety-degree angle to their upper arm, which is hanging down close to their torso. Clamping one hand on their bicep, hold their forearm behind the wrist with your other hand, and tell your partner very explicitly, "I'm going to bend your arm. Try as hard as you like to stop me; I'm going to bend your arm." Then pull the forearm back to the upper arm and you will generally have no problem bending their arm. Next, position their arm in the original V shape again, and (this is important) say to them, "Okay, forget all that. Now your forearm is a ray gun. A powerful ray of white light shines out of your fingertips. Wherever you point your forearm, the white light follows." Find a point in the room that their fingertips are generally pointing to while the arm is crooked. Then give them these precise instructions: "Now, no matter what happens, keep your forearm straight so that you keep shining white light on that point." Try bending their arm again while they follow this instruction. You will find that even with great exertion you likely will not succeed—their arm will not bend.

(For a video demonstrating the *Unbendable Arm Exercise*, please go to williamwhitecloud.com/naturalsuccessbonus/

It really is an amazing demonstration. In my seminars, participants are blown away by their own, and other people's, ability to be so powerful, even when placed in what they would assume is a physically and mechanically untenable position. If you try it out for yourself, you will no doubt be similarly impressed, especially when you realize that successfully keeping the arm straight has nothing to do with what you believe it takes—physical strength. Each result—the arm bending or not—is entirely determined by the different messages the one trying to bend the arm gives. In the first instruction, the message is clear: "I'm going to bend your arm." And the arm bends. But the second instruction pointedly does not mention anything about the arm bending. All that is suggested is the end result, and in spite of the arm bender using all their strength to bend the other person's arm, it remains rigidly straight.

When you understand the function of consciousness, you appreciate that *Natural Success* depends on your *Subconscious* saying "Yes" to messages that reflect your highest potential. There is only one aspect of you that is capable of supplying those messages: your *Super Conscious*. Learning to connect with and operate from your own personal *Genius* is the name of the game. Before you can do that, you have to be able to hear what your *Unconscious* is saying to you. And before you can do that, you have to know yourself. We're going to go on a journey now. I'm sure you'll find it fascinating, and it's certainly worth the effort. Right now, you're being offered a second chance in life: the understanding that will allow you to change track from an *Unconsciously* driven life to a *Super Consciously* inspired one.

CHAPTER TWO
THE SECOND STEP OF NATURAL SUCCESS

HEARING WHAT YOUR UNCONSCIOUS IS SAYING TO YOU

The fundamental determinant of what you create in life (which you might still think of as something that happens to you) is what your *Subconscious* says "Yes" to. More than your genetic disposition, your IQ, your education, your gender, the political system you live under, the economic conditions you are subject to, or any other factor you might believe controls your life circumstances, it's the messages you give yourself, wittingly or unwittingly, that shape your experience. Consequently, you need to be able to hear what your *Unconscious* is telling you, because it's lying to you nonstop. It's constantly telling you how you don't have "it" in you to achieve the end results you desire. It's telling you what you need to do, how you need to be, in view of the fact that you don't have "it" in you.

If you're not hearing your *Unconscious* message loud and clear, in plain English or whatever your native tongue is, then it's running the show in your consciousness without you even knowing it. If you're an *Unconscious* person, you'll only experience your *Unconscious* worldview as the unwanted circumstances you always have to cope with. No matter how hard you try to improve your lot in life, your *Unconscious* will push back like an invisible tide, undermining your best intentions and efforts. Ancient philosophers used to warn against the futility of "presumptuous denial," which means thinking that you can change anything without taking into account the underlying currents working against the expression and fulfillment of your higher potential. In *Star Wars*, the alien Jedi Master Yoda warns his young protégé, Luke Skywalker, "You underestimate the power of the Dark Side." The Dark Side is synonymous with the *Unconscious* because it is the buried, hidden aspect of consciousness. And the truth is, you aren't going anywhere, creatively, without a deep appreciation of the role of the *Unconscious* generally, or the characteristics of your own specifically.

THE POWER OF THE DARK SIDE

My younger brother, Tony, is BBQ supervisor and master of ceremonies at all our family gatherings, always living up to his role with a ready supply of jokes pertinent to any circumstance or conversation. His wry sense of humor is very endearing. But not so funny is another characteristic of his: a startling proclivity for attracting life-threatening accidents. One time he was having a drink at a suburban pub in Johannesburg, the gold mining capital of South Africa. As he and his friends enjoyed a few ales and listened to live music in the beer garden, a gang of teenage hooligans was going around the parking lot undoing the wheel nuts on every car. Later that evening, the pub patrons were in for a rude surprise when their wheels started coming off as they steered their cars around the corners of the dark suburban streets. Fortunately, none of them were hurt because of the low speeds they were doing. Tony, however, lived out in the country and was going around a bend at sixty miles an hour when all four wheels of his car flew off. He spent six months in traction, his entire body encased in plaster, like Wile E. Coyote after a run-in with the Road Runner.

Another time, he was wheeling his garbage bin out onto the street on garbage night. Like many South Africans, Tony and his family live in a fortified house behind spiked gates and walls festooned with razor wire. As he wheeled his bin through their twin-car garage, he clicked on the remote that cranked up the roller door and depressed the row of anti-theft spikes across the threshold. Just like he had a hundred times before, he ducked his head under the retracting door and stepped outside. His right foot came down on the threshold at the exact moment the anti-theft spikes decided to malfunction and release again. One of the spikes speared through his foot, nearly slicing it in half. As he lay on a gurney in the ER shortly after, he listened to two attending doctors debating whether they should try to reconstruct his mangled foot or simply cut it off. In the end they decided by flipping a coin. Luckily for my brother, the coin toss resolved in favor of reconstructive surgery.

My family and I are used to this sort of thing happening to Tony. Half of the time I've spent with him in adulthood has been by his side in hospital wards where he lay recovering from heart attacks and food poisoning and near-fatal jellyfish stings (yes, those suckers can kill you). But the curious distinction that became obvious over time is that it *only* happens to him when I visit the family back in South Africa. And, that it happens *every* time I visit. I remember calling Tony a few years ago to tell him about an impending trip. Though he made a joke of it, I could hear the alarm in his voice. "Please don't come," he begged facetiously, pointing out the bad luck my presence always brings him. I laughingly suggested it might be safer for him to visit me in Australia. "I don't think I can afford the medical bills there," he retorted humorlessly.

There is a very good explanation for this pattern of experience, even though it is also quite sad. Tony was born when I was five years old, and little me didn't appreciate him taking my place as the center of attention in my world. My mother recalls finding me one day looking into his cot and hissing venomously, "I hate you," over and over again. From when he was born until he was five, I was as cruel and mean to him as the devil torturing a soul in hell. More lately, I look at pictures of my little brother from that time and I see the keen intelligence in his eyes, along with a warm, endearing sparkle. I still cringe with shame to think how mercilessly I tormented that sweet and innocent boy, bent as I was on extinguishing his light.

Tony was saved from me only because he developed an extremely vulnerable condition whereby even a light tap to the head could have killed him. Though he eventually made a full recovery, he was out of bounds to me for many years. I couldn't even look at him the wrong way, let alone touch him, without risking a thrashing from my father. Tony had finally found a way of protecting himself from my bullying—by being mortally fragile.

In reality, Tony hasn't needed to protect himself from me for forty years or more. The antagonism between us died once we were at boarding school together, and we've been close friends all of our adult lives. But it's an *Unconscious* dynamic. To this day, whenever I appear on the scene, Tony miraculously winds up an invalid for the duration of my stay. I was hopeful that his dysfunctional pattern of self-preservation would cease once we had identified it. That has not been the case, however. The last time I was in East London, the coastal city my mother and brothers live in, I was pleasantly surprised when it was Tony who picked me up from the airport. As we drove away from the arrivals area, I was thinking that the spell must be broken, seeing as how he wasn't in hospital this time. That notion was immediately dispelled. Tony turned to me and very matter-of-factly said, "By the way, I'm going in to hospital tomorrow for heart surgery. My pacemaker failed and they have to replace it."

Never underestimate the power of the *Dark Side*! The *Unconscious* is a force to be reckoned with; it can invisibly subject us to crippling states of existence. Tony's unconscious pattern of attracting life-threatening conditions at the exact time of my visits isn't at all remarkable to me. I've seen way more spectacular dynamics than that, even. For example, I knew a lady whose father had died after a tragically protracted blood-related illness when she was very young, and since then every man she ever fell in love with ended up dying of a blood-related condition. Another friend of mine had a father who would regularly abandon the family while she was growing up. He'd disappear for months and even years, and then come back again whenever he was down on his luck. Each time, the family would take him in, feed him, love him, finance him, and then, inevitably, heartbreakingly, as soon as he was on his feet again he would be gone. Now in adulthood, my wonderfully sweet friend has an amazing talent for finding men who are completely broken and beyond redemption, and nurturing them into spectacular success stories. But of course, you know how every one of those stories ends, too.

If anything should convince us of our phenomenal creative power, it's our dysfunctional patterns—the way in which we effortlessly create the most amazing recurring experiences to perpetuate what we believe about ourselves, others, and life. Most people don't see it that way, though. Mainly because they very rarely see their patterns going all the way back to the point of origin, if they see them at all. They don't see or take responsibility for what they have *Unconsciously* created, which also means they fail to see that they have the power to manifest something equally amazing in favor of their wildest dreams, something that is an expression of their greater nature and purpose. As long as you can't see what's going on under the hood of your consciousness, you won't ever appreciate that you make it all up—like my brother made up that he has to protect himself from me by being critically injured, or that the lady I just mentioned made up that any man she loves will die of a blood-related illness—and that you can just as easily make up another story, one that reflects your true worth and power. If you know what you're doing.

INDIVIDUATION

The reason our *Unconscious* has so much power—to the point that we don't even see that there might be something else other than the reality we're used to experiencing—is because it's the aspect of consciousness that's tasked with creating our illusion of separation. The unconscious reality that we're typically subject to is an existential necessity. As *Pure Creative Spirit* connected to everything through all time and space, we come to Planet Earth for an individual experience of existence. When we're born we don't have any sense that we are *not* one and the same as our mother or the rest of our environment. While you may have to accept the *Pure Creative Spirit* concept as a premise, for now, the latter is an established psychological fact. We have to manufacture our sense of individuality via a process referred to, very obviously, as *Individuation*. Understanding the concept of *Individuation* is the key to unraveling the illusory sense of limitation we experience in our mortal guise.

As *Pure Creative Spirit*, we have to have a vehicle that can get us around in three-dimensional, physical reality. Our *Ego* is that vehicle. A common misconception is that the *Ego* is some self-centered aspect of the rational mind. In fact, it's our whole Earthly vehicle, including our physical, mental, emotional, and energetic (or etheric) bodies. People often talk about the *Ego* as if it's this evil side of us that we need to eliminate. In truth, as with the *Subconscious*, moral equations don't apply to the *Ego*. Again, it's simply our *Earthly* vehicle. The day we get rid of it is the day we leave this fair planet.

One of the *Ego's* principle functions is to serve as the vehicle of our orientation. Not only is it responsible for containing us here, it's also responsible for navigating us through our life's journey. As such, the *Ego* is dedicated to the assumption that *there is a way things are* here on Planet

Earth, definitively and absolutely. It is driven to resolve a central tension, to answer a singular question: *How is it?* The answer to that question is more important to the *Ego* than anything else. If it were given a choice between knowing how it is and having air to breath, the *Ego* would choose knowing how it is. Once it concludes how it is, the *Ego* becomes fixed in that assumption. That's because without consistency of knowledge, there is no solid orientation.

You can see why so many people have been murdered in the name of religion, which is a construct that purports to explain the meaning of our lives. Any contradiction of belief is a negation of our *Egoic* orientation, which is *Egoically* unacceptable to the degree that humans will kill to maintain or enforce the consistency of their worldview, as happens in the instance of forced religious conversions or wars. Neuroscientists have found that the same part of the brain that becomes active when our physical survival is threatened also becomes active when our beliefs are challenged. Having the answer to the question *"How is it?"* is a very big deal to the *Ego*. And it gets its answer to that all-important question by seeking validation of its own nature during the critical *Individuation Phase*, a period that lasts from the conception and formation of our physical being in the womb, through birth, and up until the age of four, maybe five.

The Maya had a beautiful proverb that speaks for many indigenous cultures' understanding of *Individuation*: "For in the child lies the future of the world: Mother must hold the baby close so that it knows that it belongs in the world; Father must take it to the highest hill so that it can see how the world is." That's very similar to another traditional adage: "Your mother lets you know you have a heart, and your father lets you know how to bring your heart into the world."

From conception until the age of eighteen months or two years old, we look to the feminine for nurturing. We want to know that we belong, that we can love and be loved. Then around the age of three or four, we look to the masculine for acknowledgement. We want to know that our actions and orientation are sound. When this validation is not met, when we aren't loved unconditionally by our mother, or acknowledged by our father, in accordance with our own sense of self, we are wounded. At some level of our being we feel pain. Our *Ego* tries to resolve the pain by making up an explanation for why we are hurting. That explanation then answers the *Ego's* question about "how it is" here, which it then holds as a fundamental belief, a rigid understanding about self, others, and the world. As you will see shortly, because these beliefs are in response to a lack of validation, they always diminish our validity, and thereby our viability, which means that we then have to develop strategies to cope with or resolve the tension that the beliefs create. Just having the beliefs puts us in a position of having to *compensate* for them in order to feel viable.

The Individuation Cycle

Pure Creative Spirit (enter egoic vehicle)

↓

Ego (vehicle of orientation) **assumes there is "a way it is".** T→R "How is it?"

↓

Ego seeks validation of Pure Creative Nature T→R
Nurturing from Mother (Feminine) 0-18 months
Acknowledgement from Father (Masculine) 3-4 years

↓

Unmet validation T→R "Why do I Hurt?"

↓

Belief

↓

Strategy to compensate for belief

*T→R = Tension Seeks Resolution

COMPENSATING LOGIC

The more you define something, the more separate you make it from everything else. Our beliefs form a set of definitions about ourselves, others, and the world. They give us a unique sense of individuality, a sense of identity. But they also give us a dysfunctional orientation in life, because we come to believe that, more than anything, we must compensate for what we believe is unviable about us. On the *Unconscious* level, we believe that this compensating for our own inadequacy is what life is all about. While the strategy we come up with to compensate, which I call our *Compensating Tendency, Strategy,* or *Logic,* creates behaviors that define our individual personalities, it also unconsciously focuses our attention on our beliefs. This *Unconscious* preoccupation or focus gives our *Subconscious* the consistent message that our lives are about our beliefs. The *Subconscious* then just says "Yes" and manifests the content of those beliefs.

One of the best definitions of *belief* I've ever come across is "*information that was useful to our survival in the past.*" As you come to appreciate belief systems and how they evolve and what they serve, you might agree that the conclusion the individuating *Ego* drew about what was going on in the *Individuation Phase*, and how best the infant self could survive it, was fair enough at the time. But outside of that context, looking back from the perspective of adulthood, those beliefs and strategies always come across as insane.

The most outrageous *Unconscious Belief* and *Compensating Tendency* I ever helped anyone uncover belonged to Petra, a young Melbourne filmmaker. In my second year of practice as an intuitive counselor, one of my clients told me about a close friend of hers who was chronically suicidal, and asked if I thought there was anything I could do for this person. On meeting Petra I immediately regretted agreeing to see her. It was plainly evident that she was medicated to the gills. She had the bloated and puffy appearance of a bovine carcass that has floated down a flooded river for a week. Her eyes were glazed over zombie-like and her lips were so swollen I wondered how she'd be able to talk. It was very disconcerting sitting there wondering how I was going to communicate with the person trapped deep inside the drooling ogre before me.

Anyway, thanks to my own focus, and to Petra being more communicative than I had given her credit for, we had a surprisingly productive session. What transpired was that her parents had been missionaries in Africa, and her father had had an affair with the housemaid while her mother was pregnant with Petra. The mission found out about the father's sinful dalliance and sent the family back to Australia in disgrace. According to her parents' religious beliefs they were not allowed to divorce, and Petra was born into a loveless environment full of shame and bitter recrimination. As an infant seeking nurturing, her *Ego* needed an explanation as to why she was getting zero validation from the feminine—or in plain human terms, why there was no love between her and her mother.

Petra's *Egoic* rationalization, we discovered, was that the problem had arisen by virtue of her mother being pregnant with Petra, meaning if Petra had not existed, the problem would not have arisen and there would still be love in the family. As a result, Petra developed the *Unconscious Belief* that her existence created the absence of love, and by that mechanical logic, her *Compensating Tendency* or *Strategy* was that she should cease to exist.

Now, if you think this is far-out, welcome to the world of the *Unconscious*! If you're going to master the art of *Conscious Creating*, then prepare yourself for a journey that makes Homer's *The Odyssey* look like a walk in the park. Perhaps you'll be even more surprised to learn that I formulated this information about Petra intuitively. She was unaware of that family dynamic in her infancy. By now her parents were deceased, but she did call her older sister for confirmation of my insight. Her sister corroborated the story, and even expressed surprise that Petra didn't know about it herself.

I trust that by now you understand the importance of being able to hear what your *Unconscious* is saying to you. You may think that you're okay, that you're not subject to such dramatic or dysfunctional belief dynamics as Petra's or my brother Tony's. Well, maybe, maybe not, but the truth is that everyone has unconscious issues that keep them preoccupied with compensating for conditions that are no longer relevant in their lives and, even more creatively damning, that keep them from being aware of their *Super Conscious* input. In spite of all the therapy Petra had undergone, and the high doses of emotion-numbing medication she had taken, she still had the seemingly irrational and relentless urge to kill herself. Worst of all, the clinical control measures she was subject to had put a lid on her true nature and potential, reducing her to part-time sheltered work, all the while being under full-time psychiatric supervision. The problem, of course, was that the underlying condition had never been addressed. Once her *Unconscious* strategy was brought to light, though, the game was up. It didn't take long for Petra to transform into a fully functioning human being. She came off her medication, lost a ton of weight, and took back control of her own life. After a lifetime of being stuck in her home city, tethered to her clinical support system, she began travelling extensively, even joining my friends and me on a four-thousand-mile safari across South West Africa. I haven't heard from her in years, but the last news I had of Petra she had taken a lover and was working full-time for a state film-and-television-funding body.

THE TWELVE FUNDAMENTAL BELIEFS

You have to hear what your *Unconscious* is saying to you. But before you can hear your *Unconscious*, you have to be aware of its existence. If you can't recognize a *Belief* at work, you'll either not be aware that your *Unconscious* is talking to you, or you'll mistake its message for common sense. I'm going to introduce you to the twelve *Fundamental Belief Systems* shared by human beings in every culture and civilization on the planet. By "fundamental" I mean that no matter what diversity of form a *Belief* takes, it can be reduced down to one of twelve essential *Beliefs*. For instance, the dynamic I had with my father, which I talked about at the beginning of the book, relates in essence to *I'm Not Allowed to be Capable*; my brother Tony's strategy to protect himself from me is *I'm Not Safe* (i.e., about *Trust*); and Petra's pathological compulsion to kill herself stemmed from an extreme case of *I Don't Belong*. You will soon become familiar with these three *Fundamental Beliefs*, as well as the other nine.

Following is a list of the *Beliefs*, accompanied by a breakdown of what they seek to compensate for or resolve and the strategies and behaviors they promote. Once you are awakened to their existence, you become more sensitive to their insinuations. This helps you hear the creatively low-level rubbish your *Unconscious* is telling you and therefore what is behind the limited, unwanted dynamics you have been creating in your life.

"I'm Unworthy" (most prevalent belief)
Seeking: *Self-referential love and approval*

Strategies:

- Seeking approval/harmony, but then rejecting the same, as receiving it would contradict the belief of being unworthy.
- Unconsciously arranging to be rejected, as this proves there's nothing about you worth loving.
- Taking steps to attract love and to belong by trying to please others.
- Taking everything personally—everything you hear is about you. This may manifest as extreme sensitivity or paranoia: "How does this relate to me?" "What does that say about me?" "What do they mean (about me), by that?"
- Becoming the center of a controversy, being dramatic or a martyr. This tests your worth, and answers the question, "How much do people accept me?"
- Setting high standards and punishing yourself relentlessly.

- Doing things a "worthy" person would do. For example, being a good Christian, environmentalist, or human rights activist, not because you truthfully care about these, but because they are what you think others consider to be worthy.
- Leaving situations such as jobs or relationships before others find out how unworthy you are.
- Using collusion, which in this case means enrolling people in your own virtues and the shortcomings of others.

"I'm Not (Good) Enough" (fairly common)
Seeking: *Wholeness*

Strategies:
- Compulsive trying. The goal is to become whole through success and hard work. Anything that is done easily is suspect.
- Over-achieving. A lot of high flyers have this belief and burn out. Often people with this belief are perpetual students and collect lots of degrees. You keep trying because you're good but not good enough.
- Often setting up achievements that don't get acknowledged. If you received acknowledgement the belief would be contradicted.
- Always looking to better yourself—enough is never enough.
- Future-orientated—always rushing ahead. "Yes...yes...go on." Future orientation can make this belief easy to see.
- Lots of "shoulds"—"I should do this, then I'll be..."
- Characterized by feelings of emptiness.

"I Don't Belong" (fairly common)
Seeking: *Identity—"Who am I?"*

Strategies:

- Launching a pre-emptive strike of being odd, weird, or different before other people kick you out (because you don't belong).
- Acting like a hermit—even among people.
- Trying to ensure having a place where you belong—"What's my place? What's my role?"
- Doing things so you won't be thrown out, rejected. People in this mode are often very likeable.
- Becoming part of, or instigating, a group, club, or cult. This is so you have somewhere to belong.
- Being hypervigilant about people—"Those people are not like us."
- Prevent being thrown out or rejected by being archly conformist, or by being so eccentric that people don't know how to react.

"I Need to Control Myself" (fairly common)
Seeking: *Orientation (Sanity)*

Control is often a strategy to support other beliefs; for instance, where someone does not TRUST their children to behave properly, they might control their kids by imposing strict rules on them. In this case, however, as a Fundamental Belief, the person believes that if they let themselves go, they will lose orientation and thereby lose their sanity.

Strategies:

- Limiting input/output so you won't get overwhelmed.

- Intellectualizing, spacing out, becoming confused, numb, or detached, or perhaps also affecting others in these ways. May also seduce or distract in order to gain control.
- Limiting thoughts, feelings, and actions to what you can control. *Coping* gives you a sense of control.
- Spending a lot of time in your head.
- Avoiding taking risks. Seeking rules. Often the rules are "should nots"—"If I know what the rules are, then I can remain in control."
- Manipulating self to *hold things together*. Setting up strategies to not go crazy—"If I don't control myself, I might not stop eating/drinking/smoking/being violent."
- Acting *out of control* as a strategy to get others to step in and force control—because you can't control yourself.
- Shortsighted (often literally)—you only see what you can control or keep together.
- Always creating a vision of negative consequences—all the terrible things that might happen if you were to take a certain course of action. You often have to manipulate yourself into taking action.

"I Can't Trust Myself, Others, or the World"
(very common)

Seeking: *Viability (sense of future), survival, safety, avoidance of violation*

Strategies:
- Cheating, being dishonest—often by not saying what you think rather than lying, because expressing your intentions directly may get you hurt.

- Unconsciously setting up others to fail and then feeling betrayed. This is a pre-emptive strike. It fulfills the assumption that others will fail you, and gives you a reason to keep your heart closed.
- Not allowing others to help you feel safe. Trying to *go it alone*. You will often feel misunderstood—"In order to survive, I have to be separate."
- Being very careful. Always seeking safety before taking action. "If I open my heart, I'll die."
- Setting up a lot of tests for people and things. Because the tests involve sabotage, this will often destroy what you want.
- Looking for trustworthy symbols—authority, mentor, teacher, etc. Once found, you will test them to find out why or where they are untrustworthy.
- Demanding guarantees and making rules, all designed to create predictability and safety.
- Getting into situations not worthy of commitment. For example, a bad relationship or hanging around with the wrong crowd.
- Commitment equates to entrapment and is akin to death. Probably why you are *always* late!
- Making plans or creating expectations involving others without telling them. If the other person doesn't come through, you feel ripped off and cheated.
- Feeling unseen, unrecognized, under-valued, violated, betrayed, ripped off.
- Often people with trust issues are open about it—"You can't trust people, you know."

"I'm Insignificant/Invisible" (a variation/strategy of Trust)

Seeking: *Viability (sense of future), survival, safety, avoidance of violation*

> As with Trust, Insignificant/Invisible does not feel safe, but specifically because of the person's feeling that others literally can't see them.

- Detaching.
- Never speaking up or asking for what you want.
- All the same characteristics of Trust.

"I Don't Have the Capacity"

To the untrained eye, this belief can look a lot like I'm Not Enough, *because it's a very active dynamic. The difference is that* Capacity *does not follow through or endure well. To appreciate* Capacity, *it helps to understand the origins of the belief, which is mainly Father derived. The individuating child, who wants acknowledgement from the Masculine, knows their Father wants something from them but never gets a clue as to exactly what that is. They get neither negative nor positive validation; it's ambivalent. Consequently, the child is not confident that they have the capacity to create. They're not sure that they get it, that they have it.*

Seeking: Scope—"How big is the game?"

Strategies:

- Gathering resources. If you have *Capacity* issues, you believe you need to expand your resources to get the job done. You get very excited about outer resources, such as technology, cars, power tools, money, and so forth, and will spend time and energy collecting these, assuming that when you have enough resources you will get what you want.

- Always assuming and suggesting that you don't have the capacity, like enough time, for example. You'll unconsciously arrange things so that you have an enormous amount to do, and thus manifest the belief.
- Trying to overcome the odds; blitz it before time runs out.
- Only trying things you already know how to do.
- Often controlling of physical space and environment.
- Getting overwhelmed, over-committed, or under-involved.
- Possibly considering yourself to be not very smart (as mental capacity is a resource), and expressing or feeling that you have missed the point of whatever is going on. This can lead to a dependence on "expert" advice, as you are unable to rely on your own understanding.
- Part of the *Capacity* belief is that you don't "get it" or that you haven't "got it"—that you don't understand something or that you don't have the desirable traits others do. Consequently, the *fear of missing out* (FOMO) on something great is big with you. This often leads to difficulty with decision-making, and a tendency to be very passionate about something one minute and totally bored with it the next.
- Talking big but not delivering when it comes to the crunch, as delivering something tangible might expose that you haven't "got it."
- Getting confused, bewildered, and unsure.
- Often becoming afraid of other people finding out that you are lacking in resources—so you'll put on a big front (you can often be very charming), but hold people at a distance when it comes to real intimacy.

"There Is a 'Right Way'"
Seeking: *Predictability*

Strategies:

- Being intolerant of deviation—trying to establish the right way.
- Being process orientated—having a rigid commitment to one way of doing things. Will focus on how it is getting done, rather than whether it's getting done or what is getting done.
- Doing things the "wrong" way and using this as an excuse for failure because you didn't follow the right way.
- Placing belief in methods, systems,—isms—often to extremes.
- Obsessing about sin—following dogmas.

"There Is a Way Things Are (a Way the World Is)"
Seeking: *Certainty and knowledge of how to be, the owner's manual to life.*

While There Is a Right Way *is about how things are done, this is about how things "are." It's a more philosophical or metaphysical tension to understand what it's all about.*

Strategies:

- Being a fundamentalist.
- Seeking knowledge—the more knowledge you have, the more you know how things operate. Then you'll know what to do and what you want.
- Reading and studying metaphysics and thinking it matters (metaphysics here meaning the ultimate nature and purpose of existence).

- Manipulating self and others based on how you think "it" is.
- Giving up responsibility of your life to the universe, God, or whatever your theory of "the way things are" is.
- Promoting your belief to save other people who don't understand "the way it is," or to bolster your theory.
- Seeking, or maybe writing, the "owner's manual to life."
- Being under-involved with others.

"I'm Powerless" (very common)
Seeking: *Outward/external results (symbols of power)*

Strategies:
- Defining yourself by accruing symbols of power (big black cars and gold chains, for example). Often people with this belief appear very powerful. Once symbols are obtained, the game becomes how to keep them (because you are powerless).
- Characteristically being angry.
- Setting up power bases to overpower people. "I've got to get them before they get me."
- Setting up circumstances to be a victim. Blaming others for what happens to you. "It's not fair." The strategy of the victim is to get saved by the person with the power.
- Assigning the power outside of yourself—"I can't do it. It's not my fault."
- Often colluding with others to seek support for your viewpoint: "It's not my fault, is it?"

- Manipulating people in order to get what you want. (Assumption is that others have the power.)
- Either acting power hungry or as a victim, because of the assumption of personal powerlessness.
- Unconsciously setting up situations to fail or lose— "I don't have the power to get what I want."

"I'm Not Allowed to Be Capable"
Seeking: Freedom to do/have what one really wants.

While you may experience this belief as "I'm not capable," in fact, more accurately, you don't believe you're allowed to be.

Strategies:

- Setting up things so that you can act incapable.
- Raising the goal posts before reaching them.
- Underachieving compared to your real capabilities. Appearing less capable than you really are.
- Avoiding situations where capabilities will or might be tested.
- Having lots of "coulds"—could do this or could do that, but never sure. Spinning wheels going nowhere.
- Constantly preparing and very process orientated, but don't actually get anything done. Always finding inessential activities to waste your time on.
- Struggling with direction.
- Lacking of commitment.

> **"I Need to Be Perfect"**
> **Seeking:** Peace, relief, and resolution
>
> *Rather than being about perfectionism, this is a belief that one needs to be perfect in essence. The belief also assumes that there is such a thing as perfection.*
>
> **Strategies:**
>
> - Often seeking purity of body, mind, and emotions. Endless fasts and cleanses.
> - Never beginning.
> - Finding fault with other people so that personal imperfection will be okay.
> - Compulsive pickiness and faultfinding, in general.
> - Being righteous.
> - Preparing to an excessive degree.
> - Destroying things before being found out to be imperfect.

UNCONSCIOUS REACTION

Here's the thing: your *Unconscious* is always telling you a bunch of creatively low-level rubbish. Whatever situation you are in, whether you've been pulled over by the cops for speeding or you're at home watching a show on TV, your *Ego* is on the alert, trying to orientate you. It's just trying to help. Unconsciously, it's asking, *"How is it?"* But instead of connecting with the relevant factors at play in the present moment (which your *Super Conscious* does), your *Ego* refers to your *Unconscious Belief System* for the answer. Essentially, it checks against your past experience to understand what is going on now.

By referencing your *Beliefs*, the *Ego* does not offer functional solutions relevant to your current situation, but instead looks at what it believes is unresolved about you, and proposes making up for that deficiency as the primary response to the situation. That's its formulaic response. It has no faith in your *Natural Ability* to viably navigate your circumstances. Using the example of being pulled over by the police, say, someone with *Worthiness* stuff might go into approval-seeking, seductive behavior; another person with *Powerlessness* issues might try to intimidate the cops by dropping the names of people in high places; if it was *Trust*, they might offer a bribe, or speed off in fear of their life. When you're not consciously aware of and in your own power, and are therefore compensating for a dysfunctional belief, you're going to make everything personal, specifically about what you believe is lacking in yourself, rather than deal with things appropriately according to the dictates of each unique situation. This is what I call an unconscious reaction.

Two very good friends of mine, Phil and Esther, bought a block of land next door to me in a new suburban development. He was a maker of fine furniture; she was a high school art teacher. Combining their considerable artistic sensibilities with their love of Eastern philosophy and, more specifically, their passion for Asian architecture, they had come up with an inspirational design for their future home. It really was set to become the model of environmental and aesthetic advancement in our neighborhood. They jubilantly put in their application for a building permit around the same time as I did.

My application was granted; theirs was refused. I forget the exact grounds on which our town council declined them, but one reason had to do with their septic waste disposal system. Before this, I had always known Phil to be a levelheaded guy who got things done using ingenuity and persistence. Now I got to see a side of him I'd never seen before. Instead of directly addressing the planning engineers' concerns, my good friend began complaining to whomever would listen about how unfair the council's decision was. His grumbling brought him into the orbit of every other disgruntled ratepayer in our county, and he was soon caught up in the small-town collusion about corruption and inefficiency in local government, especially concerning the planning department. Phil and his fellow malcontents met in coffee shops to discuss the latest whisperings of bribes, preferential treatment of relatives and friends, and big-time developments going up in clear violation of planning and building regulations. A series of angry petitions agitating for better council governance began making the rounds, and libelous letters on the subject appeared in local papers, with Phil's hand visible in all of them.

Six months after we had lodged our applications to build, construction was starting on my house while Esther and Phil's project was at a standstill. I felt sorry for Esther because her impression, along with everyone else's, was that her and Phil's design had been categorically rejected. Phil's energy had become entirely diverted to anti-corruption campaigning. One evening I was astonished to see him on the six o' clock news, fulminating about some state-level corruption issue concerning a development six hundred miles away from where we lived. Like a seventeenth-century inquisitor flushing out witchcraft and devil worship from under every stone, Phil had graduated to uncovering a nationwide web of political corruption.

It was painful to watch. The targets of Phil's attacks were far more influential and well-resourced than he was. They pushed back hard, using the full weight of the media and the law. Hardly a day went by that he wasn't being publicly ridiculed or threatened with defamation proceedings. He stood to be ruined in every way. My once jovial and gregarious friend had become the caricature of a harried man, darting in and out of courthouses, post offices, and radio stations, never having time to stop for more than a few moments to complain about the dark forces he was up against. As for poor Esther, she became a melancholy specter, stooped by the weight of the political onslaught brought on by her husband's actions.

One day I was sitting in a coffee shop chatting to a

friend. Phil approached our table, his demeanor gaunt and distracted. He had no time for pleasantries. "What do you think?" he grunted, shoving a pile of creased pages covered in his spidery scrawl under my nose. His eyes did not meet mine. He looked around nervously as if he was expecting to be ambushed.

I looked the first couple of pages over. They constituted an articulate defense of his right to speak out in the public interest. But I couldn't read any further. I pushed the scraps of paper away. "What do you want, Phil?" I asked him bluntly.

He said something like, "To hold the bastards accountable."

"No," I insisted, "what do you really want? You and Esther were going to build your dream home once. How's this all helping get that done?"

Phil stood frowning for a while. Then, he snatched up his draft letter and tore it into little pieces right in front of me and stalked out of the café without saying a word. I don't know what he and Esther talked about when he got home, but the next day she made an appointment to meet with Nigel, the chief engineer at the town council. The way Esther tells the story, she put on some makeup and a short dress and drove over to the council chambers. Nigel showed her into his office and offered her a seat. She pulled the rejected building application out of her bag and came straight to the point. "Nigel, can you explain to me exactly what we have to do to get our application approved?" Nigel explained the adjustments that needed to be made. Esther assured him that the house would accommodate his specifications. Nigel organized for the application to be approved that same day.

Esther finally took the true action that Phil should have taken right from the beginning. She established what the problem was and created a functional solution, which in this case meant complying with council directives. Blindingly obvious and straightforward, I hear you say? But never to the *Ego*. For Phil, whose primary belief is *I Need to Be Perfect*, when he received the rejection notice, he *Unconsciously* decided that his essence had been made wrong, and that accordingly he had to compensate for that perceived unviable condition by making his supposed detractors even more wrong. That was his unconscious reaction. Without realizing it, he had been drawn into a battle of righteousness, in the expectation that winning this war would get him what he wanted. In actual fact it nearly ruined him personally, never mind his chances of creating the home of his dreams. Not only were members of the town council growing more ill-disposed to Phil with every slur he hurled their way (which is why Esther had to go in and talk to Nigel), but also if his campaign had carried on any longer he would inevitably have been bankrupted by a slew of mounting lawsuits. As it happened, because he was well enough trained in the principles of *Natural Success*, Phil was able, with my prompting, to recognize and snap out of his dysfunctional preoccupation and change track back to taking action in favor of his truly desired end result.

An interesting footnote in Phil's story is that once he was back on track with building his home, he lost all interest in his anti-corruption crusade. In truth, it had nothing to do with what actually mattered to him. One day he and I were about to go into the same coffee shop where I had called him on his racket, when he spotted a group of his former co-conspirators around a table. "Let's go somewhere else," he muttered in true Aussie style, "these ratbags give me the shits."

Learning to manage our reactions is key to operating on a *High-Level Creative Frequency* in life. When we don't have the discipline or the tools to examine our psychological tensions, we miss the opportunity to hear what our *Unconscious* is telling us, and when we miss what our *Unconscious* is telling us, that message goes straight into our *Subconscious* unchecked and unopposed. Without even being aware of it, we are drawn into the *Have Not* worldview and compensating behaviors of our *Egoic* belief system. Imagine the time and anguish Phil could have saved himself and Esther and all those he involved in his six-month-plus drama had he consciously addressed the charged emotions confronting him when he originally got the bad news from the town council. I've never met the person who actually believed what their *Unconscious* was telling them. Had he stopped to listen to what his bruised thoughts and feelings were effectively saying, Phil would not have gone along with the ideas that the council's rejection of his building plan meant that he was personally flawed and that if he proved the authorities to be even more flawed than himself he would get what he wanted.

THE POWER OF HANGING OUT WITH TENSION

Please pay close attention to what I'm going to say next. This is one of the most important creative insights you'll ever receive. Earlier I mentioned that societally we are subject to a set of misconceptions that work against our existential aspirations in the same way that a tidal current works against the floundering swimmer. Right at the top of that list, head and shoulders above the rest, is the perception that tension is bad. We live in an extremely conflict-averse society that assigns a negative value to emotional discomfort. In the old days, messengers who brought bad news to kings and army commanders were put to death. And even to this day, anyone who points out an uncomfortable truth is quickly silenced and made to feel bad.

Little Johnny says out loud, "Why does Granny smell funny?"

Mummy snaps, "Don't be rude, Johnny." To Granny she says, "Sorry, Granny, Johnny is going through a rude phase. Aren't you, Johnny? Saying the most ridiculous things!"

Personally, I think our *Tension Phobia* finds its most overreaching expression in the *Positive Thinking* movement. A plethora of Personal Development modalities subscribe to *Positive Thinking*, either as the sole basis of their model or as a key principle within it. What *Positive Thinking* assumes is that negative thoughts and feelings will be picked up by the *Subconscious* and attracted into reality, so they therefore have to be denied and replaced with positive thoughts and feelings. This premise is usually based on an incomplete understanding of how consciousness works.

There are two things you have to understand about consciousness before you can wield it masterfully. Firstly, your thoughts and feelings don't express actual reality; they are the spokespersons of your *Unconscious Beliefs*, something we will look at in more depth later. They have no power unless you give them the power. Secondly, your *Subconscious* is not relying on your thoughts and feelings alone for direction, which *Positive Thinking* assumes. Your *Subconscious* also receives input from your *Super Conscious*, another subject we will explore more fully later. For now, just know that your *Subconscious* doesn't simply receive one message at a time in a linear sequence; it's actually simultaneously subject to a variety of conflicting messages. In order to know which message to engage, it looks at which message has the power—which message is being given the most energy—and creates that one.

As a simplistic example, imagine you are in a bar and your attention is drawn to someone you find attractive. A conflict develops in your mind. Your spontaneous *Super Consciously* inspired impulse is to go over and introduce yourself. Countering that, you feel a sense of trepidation and a voice in your head tells you that you're not good enough for that person, that they will spurn you. Your *Subconscious* is observing this back-and-forth between your passionate impulse and your unconscious *Worthiness* issue without any bias. Only once it gets a sense of which input has the power does it say "Yes" to that message and manifest it as reality. What eventuates between you and that hot-looking person sitting across the room depends on which message you choose to go along with.

The fact of the matter is that *Positive Thinking* does not actually work for most people. I know. I've been told by thousands of people in seminars and on talk-back radio. They tell me that it's not working and they ask me what they're doing wrong. What they're doing wrong is practicing *Positive Thinking*. Experiencing unwanted circumstances, putting a positive spin on them, and then expecting that reframe of reality to translate into a fabulous outcome is just presumptuous denial, and doesn't actually change anything. We all know that saying: "What you resist persists." Of course it does. When you resist your negative thoughts and feelings, when you deny or pretend that they don't exist, you're doing so because you believe they have the power. You're actually in reaction. By resisting your unwanted thoughts and feelings, you're giving the beliefs they speak for the power, so of course your reality will continue to reflect them. Powerful people don't need to fabricate positivity, they *are* positive by virtue of the fact that they are not threatened by negativity—their own or others'. They can hang out with tension.

The first time I ever really grasped the meaning of true power was back in my poorer days, when a friend of mine and I were raising money for an ambitious community theatre project. Another friend of ours was dating a very successful property developer and she suggested we come to a party her boyfriend was throwing and talk to him about making a donation. Arriving at this party was like walking into a scene from *The Great Gatsby*. Mercedes Benzes and Bentleys and Ferraris and Porsches lined our prospective benefactor's half-mile-long driveway. As we neared the house, blonde girls in miniskirts and hot pants with legs up to their necks milled around smoking joints and giggling at the braggadocious banter of sharply dressed young men. The balconies and halls of the mansion thronged with well-heeled revelers. Giddy laughter filled the air. All the floors were sticky with spilled champagne. Women squatted in the shadows of the garden because they couldn't get into the toilets full of people doing lines of cocaine.

With my old beat-up car parked out of sight, and me looking about as glamorous as an off-duty policeman, I couldn't remember feeling more out of place or self-conscious in my whole life. I could tell that Theo, my fundraising partner, was equally ill at ease. The only way we differed was in how we each dealt with our social awkwardness. I withdrew and became an observer; he attacked the booze and, then, emboldened by the vodka and tequila, muscled his way into the bathroom to powder his nose. By the time we were summoned for an audience with our host, Theo was visibly unhinged. To say that I was panicked by my friend's intemperate condition is an understatement.

Shuffling into Paul the multimillionaire's plush study, cap in hand as it were, was like switching between the sets of *The Great Gatsby* and *The Godfather*. Paul sat behind his dining table–size desk regarding us impassively. Unlike everyone else at his party, he was stone-cold sober. Only after we had been standing before him dumbly for several minutes did he wave us into the seats on our side of the desk. I gathered from his fleeting expression of contempt that it was a mark against us that we needed his permission. There was another uncomfortable pause during which he summed us up with sharp, calculating eyes. When he finally spoke, it was with that same air of dismay that he needed to take the initiative. Though he said, "So what can I do for you?" it sounded more like, "Let's get this waste of time over with."

I looked at Theo to indicate that I would do the talking. But he jumped in ahead of me and, to my consternation, proceeded to tell Paul what he thought of him, in the most uncomplimentary terms. He savagely denounced our prospective donor as a narcissistic sociopath who operated in life by preying on others' weakness for his own selfish gain. He evidently had quite a bit of dirt on the developer, obviously obtained from the man's own lover, seeing as though she featured prominently as the main case in point. As he ranted, Theo's face contorted hideously. Flecks of spit rained like sleet from his mouth, and the moustache of white powder under his nose exaggerated his vulgar demeanor. In my mind I pictured our much-counted-upon donation going up in smoke.

I interrupted Theo, hoping it would silence him and appease Paul at the same time. "Ha, ha, ha," I chuckled, "he's a kidder. C'mon, Theo, let's get serious. The man's got a party to host."

But Theo was having none of it. "No," he objected forcefully, "this guy's evil, man." He began impressing on me what a dark, Machiavellian individual we were dealing with. I tried to pacify him. We went back and forth in an excruciating exchange, with my attempts to keep the peace only escalating Theo's determination to paint Paul's character in the worst possible light.

To my surprise, the man whom I was trying to defend put an end to our squabble by pointing at me and barking, "Why don't *you* shut up, man? This guy is trying to speak his mind, and you're doing all you can to shut him up. Goddamn let him have his say."

I was both devastated and dumbfounded to find myself the alienated party. Disarmed by Paul's openness, Theo's harangue transitioned into more of a well-intentioned feedback, which his erstwhile nemesis listened to with keen interest. The tycoon gazed steadfastly at Theo, nodding his head softly in admission at the points being made, at times wincing when they hit home hard. When at last Theo had exhausted his character assessment, Paul's response was sincere. "Spot on, mate, thank you. It's good to know what other people honestly think about you." They left me sitting alone and mortified in the study, and walked out to rejoin the party, each patting the other warmly on the back.

We didn't get the donation we were after, but I got something far more valuable from that experience. It was the first time in my life that I had witnessed anyone be so open to such a stinging rebuke of their own person. I asked myself what quality Paul might possess that he could be so okay with that level of personal confrontation, and the answer that immediately occurred to me was *power*! *Power* being the confidence, or at least the assumption, that no matter how things seem or what others say, what a person creates is determined by the will of that person themselves and not anything else. Paul could hear or feel anything because to his mind there wasn't any condition that could limit his possibility or potential.

CONFLICT AS A TOOL FOR SELF-AWARENESS

Your thoughts and feelings are messages from your *Unconscious*, and when you resist them, you give those messages the power. There are other creative imperatives for not being so quick to dispel the tension of your painful thoughts and feelings. For a start, tension is the fuel of your creative engine, your *Subconscious* creativity, and when you see how important it is in this respect, you will quickly change your relationship with inner conflict to one of appreciation rather than aversion. But as it applies to the *Second Step of Natural Success*, conflict is the most profound tool for self-awareness you will ever come across. If approached consciously, rather than reactively, it allows you to deconstruct your whole *Unconscious* dynamic. The benefit is that the resulting insights help to neutralize the dysfunctional agendas and behaviors that are otherwise automatically in operation. This, in turn, positions you to orientate from a *Super Conscious* perspective, something that is not possible without first hearing what your *Unconscious* is telling you. This might be why the Sufis, the mystical branch of the Islamic faith, say that the dysfunctional personality is the gateway to the soul.

It's actually very easy to hear what your *Unconscious* is saying, if you're prepared to be honest with yourself. You only have to listen. I'm aware of several Creative Development modalities that use a technique I call the *Conflict Deconstruction Exercise* to uncover the *Unconscious* dynamic at play in any emotionally charged or unwanted situation. Firstly, you simply state the problem and acknowledge your wounded thoughts and feelings. Next, you look at how you are unconsciously defining yourself, others, and the world. You establish those definitions by asking yourself what you believe the problem means—viscerally, not intellectually. Then you consider what the underlying assumption is, which means: taking into account the negative situation and your limited thoughts and feelings and definitions, what is the bottom-line belief you are holding in relation to all of that? And finally, you observe, truthfully, what you are giving the power to (where you are really putting your energy and focus)—is it the end result you would love in this situation or the unconscious assumptions about where you stand in the situation? Once all of the above is apparent to you, you will also notice your maladaptive approach (your *Compensating Tendency* or *Strategy*) to resolving the tension of your unconscious preoccupation.

As an example, let's imagine Phil taking himself through the *Conflict Deconstruction Exercise* in his house-building application scenario:

> **Problem:** My building application has been rejected.
>
> **Thoughts:** That I can't get what I want. All my hard work has been thwarted and there's nothing I can do to change it. I am going to take a loss on my investment, and having our dream dashed will also have a negative effect on my relationship with Esther.
>
> **Feelings:** Sad. Frustrated. Angry. Depressed. Also feeling fear in relation to Esther.
>
> **Definition and meaning:**
>
> **Self:** I am powerless in the face of the powers that be. I can't get what I want because I'm flawed. I can never be right.
>
> **Others:** Are not flawed. They have the power. Are petty, judgmental, and critical.
>
> **The world:** Has high standards. Does not tolerate and deals harshly with imperfection. Has it in for me. Obstructs my will.
>
> **Underlying assumption:** Because I'm flawed, the world and others refuse to allow me to create anything.
>
> **What am I giving the power to?** The notion that I don't stand a chance of getting what I want.
>
> **How am I compensating for/trying to resolve all of the above?** I'm putting my energy into rebelling

and destroying the forces that I perceive oppose me, by exposing their faults.

What does my behavior obviously result in? Ever-increasing resistance to me and what I'm trying to achieve.

The vampire of mythology is a bloodsucking creature that fills our imaginations with dread. One of their most fiendish qualities is that they can't be killed as long as they operate under cover of the night. But if ever they meet the light of day they perish instantaneously and dissolve into thin air. There could not be a better metaphor for our energy-draining psychological quandaries, which I call *Emotional Tension*.

As long as we are unaware of our beliefs at work, their power builds, fueling our painful thoughts and feelings and dysfunctional behaviors. But when we bring them to light, we take the power out of them, partly because the *Self Conscious*—the awake and aware part of our consciousness—recognizes the absurdity of their proposition and conveys that repudiation to the *Subconscious*. More importantly, in creative terms, once we have recognized the *Unconscious* message, we are in a position to establish our *Super Conscious* preference and give that the power. This is the only meaningful and effective way in which we can escape the karma of our limited *Have Not* paradigm and enjoy the fruits of living life on a *High-Level Creative Frequency*, the state of being that is responsible for *Natural Success*.

CHAPTER THREE
THE THIRD STEP OF NATURAL SUCCESS

PREPARING THE FERTILE GROUND FOR YOUR GENIUS TO EMERGE

Let me say categorically: trying to clear or get rid of *Unconscious Beliefs* is a waste of time. Worse, it only gives them more energy or power. The sophisticated creator knows that the *Subconscious* is less informed by explicit statements and thought forms than it is by behavior. It is always inferring the underlying assumptions behind your actions and reactions (whether those assumptions reflect your *Unconscious Beliefs* or, as we'll be discussing, your *Super Conscious* wisdom) and being guided by those conclusions as to what it should create. When it sees you reactively polarizing against your beliefs (i.e. compensating for them because you have put the power in them), your *Subconscious* rightly concludes that you assume the beliefs have the power, and it will create a reality consistent with that conclusion.

Of course, *Self Conscious* intellectual concepts like whether there is a God or not—or if Earth is flat or round—can change. Views and opinions can easily be dispelled by contrary evidence, rational argument, peer attitudes, changed circumstances, and so on. But your *Unconscious Beliefs* formed by your wounding in the *Individuation Phase* orientate your *Ego*. Because orientation is the name of the game for the *Ego*, it has to remain faithful to those assumptions, no matter what evidence there is to the contrary. The point is, though, that you don't have to change your beliefs, you only have to change your focus. You only have to change what you put your energy in and therefore give the power to. This book deals with shifting out of the dead-end struggle of *Compensating Tendency* or *Strategy* into the ease and joy of *High-Level Creative Function*.

As we have established, *Low-Level Creative Function* is a result of being externally referenced or informed. This doesn't only mean what we take onboard from outside ourselves currently; it also includes the input of our *Unconscious Beliefs*, which were originally derived from external circumstances involving others—our mother and father, to be specific. Now we are going to learn how to tap into the *Genius* within—our own inner source of wisdom and inspiration—something that very few people on the planet know how to do with any skill or consistency.

We have all been thoroughly conditioned to believe that our highest creative faculty is not real, not valid, and that the non-rational ideas and insights that sometimes do manage to break through into our *Self Conscious* awareness are highly suspect, if not downright dangerous. This is an important lesson, therefore, and not at all like learning some facts in school, such as the dates of famous battles in history. This chapter relates to the real education we all missed out on. In order to draw out or bring forth the *Genius* that is our inherent birthright, we literally have to rescue our *Super Conscious* intelligence from the nebulous dreamscape it has been left to languish in and give it back its exalted place in the world of tangible, concrete knowledge. It falls to us to defy the societal taboos that keep us from expressing our full potential; only we can awaken this giant capacity within ourselves and transform it into the guiding principle of our lives.

BELIEF CREATES REALITY

The reason why there is such a preoccupation with belief-clearing and self-healing and fixing in the modern-day self-help movement—which includes Spiritual and Personal Development—is because of the pervading assumption that we are our wounds. But we are not our wounds. Our wounds are the chassis of the vehicle that transports who we really are through this thing called life. And, as such, they should not be tampered with. Trying to resolve our illusion of separation and limitation only distracts us from the business of living out our whole, undented, undiminished, undaunted, and infinitely creative nature.

There is no denying that it is relatively true that *belief creates reality*. As *Pure Creative Spirit* connected to everything through all time and space we enter our *Egoic Vehicle*, which seeks validation of our nature. When that need is not met in some way, we hurt. We try to resolve that pain by explaining it to ourselves, and those explanations become concretized as *Unconscious Beliefs*. We become preoccupied with our beliefs because we assume that coping with those perceived limitations is what our life is all about. That unconscious preoccupation or focus gives our beliefs the power, and they begin manifesting as our reality, both in terms of our perception and our actual experience.

Belief Creates Reality

```
         Belief
       ↗        ↘
Reinforces     Creates
       ↖        ↙
         Reality
```

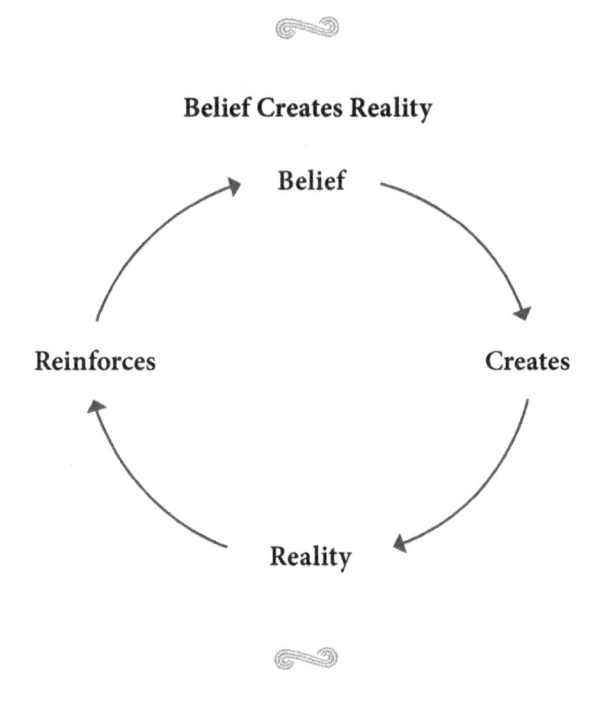

As long as our *Unconscious* dynamic has the power, then of course our *Subconscious* manifestations—what we actually create in our lives—will reflect that focus. Everyone can prove their beliefs because they play out in their lives continually. But we don't have to be caught up in this cycle of limitation. Our *Subconscious* can just as easily manifest a reflection of our *Super Conscious* potential—if we divert our attention, our focus, to this higher aspect of consciousness. Operating on a *High-Level Creative Frequency*—from our *Genius*—is not an automatic function, though; it takes *Self Conscious* action to effect that shift. And before you can take functional action in this respect, you have to be able to discern and distinguish your *Super Conscious* message from your *Unconscious* message. Here, an appreciation of the different modes of awareness that serve these aspects is crucial.

MODES OF AWARENESS

Fundamentally, we can say that there are two modes of awareness that we are informed by: *Perception*, our *Egoic* or *Unconscious* mode of awareness, and *Intuition*, our *Super Conscious* mode of awareness. By discussing *Perception* and *Intuition*, I don't just want to give you an insight into the nature of these modes and how they differ, I want to be sure that you appreciate the creative imperative of ceasing to identify with your *Perception* and starting to develop a strategic relationship with your *Intuition*. Without an understanding of how you process reality, and how you can improve the quality of that process, you remain a fish in a fishbowl without knowing it and without the means to leap into the wide-open waters of *Natural Success*. Awareness is everything.

The most astonishing story I've ever heard relating to the transition from *Unconscious* awareness to *Super Conscious* awareness is the account of how the escape fire was invented. In rural Africa where I grew up, fighting bush fires in winter was as normal as shoveling snow would be in Canada. A standard survival technique we used was controlled burns, which involved pre-emptively burning an area you could retreat into if the fire you were fighting got out of hand. It's just such an obvious tactic that I assumed the procedure had been around forever. But it turns out that the escape fire is a surprisingly modern practice, invented somewhat accidentally in the late nineteen-forties by a man with the improbable name of Wag Dodge.

Wag Dodge was a smokejumper, which is what they called the heroic Montana firemen who parachuted into rough, inaccessible terrain to fight forest fires. One day Wag and his crew of over a dozen men, of whom he was the leader, were fighting an out-of-control mountain fire fanned by a gale-force wind, which suddenly turned on them as the wind changed direction. Wag and his smokejumpers were pinned against a steep grass-covered hill by a fifteen-foot wall of flames bearing down on them at lightning speed. Terrified for their lives, they all turned and began scrambling frantically up the hill.

Their leader knew that retreat was futile. There was no chance that they could outrun the advancing inferno. Wag Dodge felt the same terror that every other member of his team could feel, and his own terror's urgent call to flee for his life. But it was also sickeningly obvious to him that running would not save them from the murderous fire breathing down their necks. If there was any way of being saved, it was not running away. And if there was a solution, it could not occur to them while they were running.

Overriding his own highly alarmed internal self-preservation system, Wag Dodge stopped in his tracks and called on his men to do the same. Though he ordered them, as their leader, to stand their ground, they ignored him, heeding rather the louder, dread-filled urging of their own terror. They continued stumbling their way up the rocky incline, desperately thrashing through the dry thatch that was fuel to the blaze that would in minutes engulf them. Wag couldn't blame them—he didn't have a better idea—just a sure certainty that if there were one, it wouldn't present itself to them in a blind panic.

As Wag looked from his deserting comrades scrambling away from him back to the giant flames closing in from behind, he suddenly realized that the answer was staring him in the face. Fire! He could set the grass where he stood alight, and if a big enough clearing could be burned off around him, he could conceivably be saved from being roasted alive. The same dry grass that was fuel to the inferno that would be the death of him could equally be his savior.

There was no chance he could catch up with the other smokejumpers and explain the plan to them. Wag had just enough time to set a match to some grass and fan the flames with his jacket. As his fire took and began blazing uphill he retreated behind it into the ashes of the burnt-out thatch. Only a few minutes later the main fire caught up with the squad leader and raged all around him, but he had burned off enough of a clearing to not be directly scorched by the monstrous flames. Not that he got off scot-free. Because he hadn't had time to burn a bigger break, he was still badly harmed by the fire. Wag ended up in hospital suffering serious burns and smoke inhalation. Nevertheless, his inspired idea to fight fire with fire had saved his life. He was one of only two smokejumpers from his team who survived that terrible conflagration.

You'll find many references to Wag Dodge's incredible story in articles and books related to creativity and intuition because it illustrates so perfectly the dichotomy between *Unconscious* and *Super Conscious* modes of awareness, as well as the process for switching from *Low-Level Creative Function* to *High-Level Creative Function*—not to mention the benefits! If you think about the story, the key to it is that when Wag stopped running he was no longer in reaction. When he literally stopped, he was no longer being driven by his charged emotions, and that is when he was able to make a connection between elements of reality that apparently no human had ever made before and formulate a lifesaving solution. Through his *Self Conscious* action, he unwittingly facilitated a shift in consciousness that led him to invent the escape fire.

THE PURPOSE AND LIMITATION OF EMOTIONS

If you intend to shift from an *Egoic* (*Low-Level Creative*) mode to a *Super Conscious* (*High-Level Creative*) mode, then you have to change your relationship to emotions, and cease identifying with them as a reflection of objective reality. What we now know, thanks to neuroscience, is that the function of emotion is to drive decisions. This was discovered with the advent of brain surgery. It was already known that the orbital frontal lobe, which is a part of the brain that sits behind our eyes, is our main emotional center. When the first operations were performed to remove cancer patients' orbital frontal lobe it was anticipated that it would be beneficial to them, not only from a lifesaving perspective, but also because it was thought that by not having emotions to cloud their judgments any longer, these individuals would become intellectually sharper. But what happened was that instead of becoming more rationally effective in life, they ended up being incapable of making the simplest of decisions, like what cereal to have for breakfast or which tie to wear to work.

To you and me these seem on the surface to be straightforward, uncomplicated considerations, but to the rational part of our brain trying to compute the most optimum way to go in any situation, there are an infinite number of variables—as illustrated by the never tiring cliché of a woman trying to decide what to wear to a party. There has to be some mechanism to force us into making a decision. And that's what we need our emotions for, to say as urgently as the occasion demands, "Bloody hell, just wear the pearl earrings," or "Why don't we have cornflakes today?" or "Fire! Run!"

Our emotions present us with the bottom line of an unconscious computation of everything we know relevant to a decision, saving us the ponderous task of analyzing all of that information consciously. Because that computation occurs outside of our *Self Conscious* awareness, we perceive it to be something we arrive at outside of our rational function, and think of it as some mysteriously independent emotional intelligence. But there is nothing irrational about the process; it's just happening instantaneously and out of sight.

While this may be a massively convenient function in many ways, and might save us from overthinking getting out of a saber-toothed tiger's way, it also comes with a serious drawback. The limitation of emotions is that they are essentially only the sum of what we know from past experience and, more damningly from a creative perspective, mainly sum up the biases formed by the same past experience. In other words, emotions are a decision-making mechanism driven by our *Unconscious Beliefs*.

The phenomenon of unconscious bias is well understood. Scientists have done many experiments devoted to this subject. One of the most widely referred to of these experiments is the blind winetasting tests where connoisseurs are told nothing about the wines they are judging other than the supposed price of each variety. So conditioned are we all with the notion of price as an indicator of quality that expert tasters uniformly judge the varieties assigned the higher prices to be the best, when in fact the prices of the superior and inferior wines have been intentionally switched.

When I was living back in Australia, a friend of mine was trying to promote an international Personal Development guru without any success. She was advised to increase the price of the workshops by more than double what she was originally charging. As soon as she took the advice, places in the workshop started selling like hot cakes. All of the fundamental reasons for making the choice not to attend the event remained the same, but evidently the increase in cost unconsciously implied an increase in the guru's worth, which skewed more prospects to "feel" like signing up. If true logic had anything to do with it, the increased price should have deterred them even more.

The Indian philosopher Jiddu Krishnamurti was once asked what he considered the biggest impediment to enlightenment. He replied, "Identification with the senses."[1] Our biggest stumbling block, creatively, is that we take our thoughts and feelings at face value as being true. We just assume that they reflect actual reality, and that whatever responses they propose are self-evidently the right ones. But our thoughts and feelings don't reflect actual reality—they reflect what we believe about reality from our past experience, and the responses they impose on us are also limited to strategies we learned in the past. Most people are startled to discover that their thoughts and feelings are not exactly relevant to whatever is occurring in any present moment. But it's true, you can't be in the now if you are identified with your thoughts and feelings, because they only reflect your past.

Again, this is why the story of Wag Dodge and the escape fire is so relevant to creativity and intuition. Everything in Wag's and his team's experience told them, through the terror they felt, that they were about to suffer the most

[1] See J. Krishnamurti, First public talk in Saaned, (July, 1978).

horrific consequences unless they took urgent action. And the only action available to them, in their experience—as conveyed to them by their fear—was to run for their lives. That adrenalin-fueled terror commanded them to flee. What is exceptional about their leader is that something in his mind intervened—some kind of spontaneous inspiration, you could say—to impress on him the nonsensical, emotionally heretical conviction that his only hope lay in not running. We can't imagine the act of will it took for Wag to stand still in the face of his reaction to the oncoming fire. What we do know, though, is that when he stopped going along with his panicked emotions, his mind was suddenly able to make a leap in logic outside of his experience, to come up with an idea that no one had ever thought of before. Wag Dodge's story is a brilliant example of how when we cease to identify with our senses—our thoughts and feelings—we create the fertile ground for our *Genius* to emerge.

DEFINITION CREATES PERCEPTION

Let me tell you another crazy story that illustrates the nature and power of *Perception*. Back in the old days on our farm, vultures circling low in the sky over the savannah meant that something on the ground was either dead or dying. One day a group of African herdsmen rounding up cattle for dipping were missing an ox from their herd. When they spotted a kettle of vultures circling close to a nearby hill, the herdsmen suspected that their missing ox might be in trouble, and a couple of them were dispatched to go and investigate. What they found, though, was not an animal but a naked tribesman lying unconscious at the foot of a big Leadwood tree with the most horrific wounds all over his body. A vehicle was called in and the man was transported to the farm infirmary, where he lay for days in a coma.

The tribesman's presence at our little bush hospital caused quite a stir. His injuries were severe: his knees and elbows were dislocated, deep lacerations covered his arms and torso and legs, and he had taken a massive blow to the crown of his head. And while he was unconscious it remained a mystery as to the cause of his grievous condition. The herdsmen who had found him were expert trackers—they could look at an antelope hoof print in the dust and tell you the species, whether it was male or female, how much it weighed, and the length of its horns—and they had found no signs that could explain what had happened. For all anyone could tell, the man may as well have fallen from the sky. The farm managers, the attending doctor and nurses, and local police waited anxiously for him to recover.

When finally the tribesman came around and was well enough to speak, the account he gave shocked everyone who had been waiting on tenterhooks to hear it. It turned out his wounds were self-inflicted. According to the man's solemn statement, he had taken a shortcut through the cattle section from a tribal settlement on one side of our farm to his own settlement on the other side. As was typical of tribesmen at that time, he was barefoot and dressed only in a java-print sarong and a jackal-skin *beshu*, a loincloth that native men usually wore over their sarongs. All he carried was his knob-kerrie fighting stick and an assegai, the short stabbing spear favored by tribal warriors. As he walked along a path meandering through the savannah woodlands, he came across a clump of guinea fowl feathers—the only remains of a recent falcon kill. He knelt down to pick out a few choice flight feathers to adorn his hair with. After making his selection he stood up again, at which moment a big black-maned lion walked out of the bush onto the path only a few steps in front of him.

The warrior froze. There was nothing else he could think to do. He hadn't even collected his weapons, which were standing against a nearby tree. The lion broke the impasse by opening its mouth wide and letting out a fearsome roar. The man turned and fled back down the path in the direction from which he had come. As he sprinted away in terror for his life, he could hear the lion running behind him. He lunged ahead, running as fast as his legs could carry him. But still he could hear the lion right behind him, and then feel its breath on his back.

In desperation the tribesman veered off the path and began crashing through the thick bush. The lion chased him into a thicket of thorn shrubs. The razor-sharp prongs stuck in his feet and gashed his body. But he couldn't stop. Now other members of the pride had joined in the chase. The warrior could hear lions on either side of him, and he fancied he caught glimpses of them out the corners of his eyes. Eventually he came across another path, which he now tore along in complete disregard of his wounds and the painful stitch developing in his side and the loss of his sarong and beshu, which had been snatched from his waist by thornbushes.

By this time the man did have a hunch that there were either no lions chasing him, or that they weren't serious about catching him. After all, his logic told him that if it had wanted to, the original black-maned male would have caught him within seconds of him starting away from it. But this reasoning was dismissed by a more palpable reality in which he really was being chased by a whole pride of lions that were constantly on the verge of catching him. Some automatic force within him forced him to keep running.

Things really started to get out of control when the new path he was on began leading down a steep hill. Now his toes stubbed on rocks and stones and he struggled to keep his balance. As he picked up speed his body got ahead of his wobbling legs and he began tumbling down the hillside. Even as he rolled head over heels he could not stop himself from running, and his knees and elbows kept bumping into the hard earth and stones, which explained why they were all dislocated. The last thing he remembered was a fierce blow cracking his skull and a fireworks display of stars going off in his mind. He had smashed headfirst into the Leadwood tree at the bottom of the hill, where the herdsmen found him lying in a coma.

I used to think this was the weirdest story I had ever heard. I knew that the uneducated tribespeople I had grown up around were very superstitious and capable of imagining the most bizarre supernatural events. It was quite normal even for a member of our domestic staff to turn up for work in the morning and matter-of-factly recount a terrifying encounter with some mythical creature during the night. But how, I asked myself, could anyone be so silly as to nearly kill themselves running away from a pride of imaginary lions? I finally got the answer when I started learning about creativity, and it has nothing to do with being silly.

We have a process in our workshops we call the *Perception Exercise*, where people sit in pairs facing each other. The facilitator asks the participants to imagine their partner embodying different qualities, like being good and then bad, or being powerful and then powerless, trustworthy and then untrustworthy, and so on. What everyone notices is how, as they keep redefining the other person, their impression of that person changes in accordance with the changing definition. If it is a positive definition, the person will appear warm and benign, pleasant-looking even, and the one defining them will feel positively disposed towards them. If it is a negative definition, the other person will appear dark and malignant, unpleasant-looking, and seem to exude a repulsive energy. These impressions vary in intensity from person to person doing the exercise, in some cases slightly, with just a mild sense of the defined quality, or in others very palpably, with a drastic difference in sentiment and strong physiological changes to match the redefined quality. Generally, everyone gets it: Our perception of reality is not based on some objective comprehension of our situation, but rather on the definitions we are holding at any given time. As I've heard it said, we don't see things for what *they* are, we see them for what *we* are.

In my trainings I also like to show a movie called *Howl's Moving Castle*, a wonderful film about magic, made by the Oscar-winning Japanese animation team Studio Ghibli. One of the features of the magician's castle is a front door that opens each time onto alternative settings: sometimes towns in different kingdoms; sometimes country fields, wastelands, battlegrounds, and night skies. Whatever world the door opens to is determined by a dial, which the castle residents set before opening the door. It's a very clever metaphor for the premise that our experience of the outer world is determined by the settings in our own consciousness—and that we have control of those settings. Of course, it's never explained what the dial in the castle actually represents—what it is that we set within ourselves that determines our reality—but with what I know about consciousness—and magic—I'm betting it's definition.

Come to think of it, that tribesman who got chased by the imaginary lions, he and his kin—including our house servants—lived in a magical world much like the one in *Howl's Moving Castle*. Their world was defined as a supernatural realm, and that was their experience of it: sorcerers snuck through their lands blighting crops and sterilizing cattle; demons rattled their roofs at night and broke down their doors to strangle them in their beds; water spirits tried to abduct them when they bathed in rivers; their enemies paid witch doctors to curse them with bad luck and pestilence, and they in turn paid other witch doctors to defend them and counter-curse their antagonists; shamans travelled to other universes to fetch back stolen fragments of their souls; everyone knew someone in their village who could turn themselves into some kind of animal; and many other things went on, some too dark to mention. They navigated a life fraught with dread and wonder.

Now I understand how a native warrior walking alone in the wilds, who is suddenly and without warning staring into the jaws of a roaring lion—the king of all predators—might unconsciously set a dial inside his mind defining himself as dead meat. And I'm not surprised that from there, with his *Subconscious* impregnated with that definition, he would begin creating a vivid reality of himself being lion prey, complete with sound, sensory, and visual effects. And that even though his logic might try to intervene and point out that the danger has passed, he couldn't switch off the scenario of being hunted, and couldn't stop running for his life even as he summersaulted down a mountainside. I've seen an antelope being chased by lions right up close, seen the frantic desperation in its eyes as it drew on every ounce of its energy to pull away from its attackers. The tribesman had become that antelope.

You might read about this native man's experience with an aloof detachment, as if you're regarding some anthropological curiosity that has no relevance to your modern, civilized mentality or experience. But just because you live in a world that is defined as a mechanical, cause-and-effect dimension and is dominated by rational, scientific principles, doesn't mean you aren't subject to the same dynamics of the Subconscious, or that you aren't using equal amounts of energy to make up equally fantastic scenarios. Trust me, you are!

Just think, if we in our technologically advanced society are capable of creating patterns of experiences like my brother Tony ending up in hospital every time I come near him, or like the woman I know who has a habit of falling in love with men about to succumb to a fatal blood-related illness, then what crazy perceptions are we not capable of forming? You are a reality-manufacturing machine. Every moment you occupy is an experience of a reality you created. As you travel through life situation by situation, your *Ego*, as the vehicle of your orientation, wants to know "How is it here?" By answering that question, it can know how to operate in that environment. The problem is that the *Ego* has no originality; it doesn't refer to the relevance of the moment—it doesn't look at the actual factors at play or the possibilities or potential in any situation. Instead, it looks at the *Unconscious Beliefs* you have that are relevant to the situation, and it communicates those beliefs to you through your thoughts and feelings. Your thoughts and feelings form a perception of what the reality of the situation is. Unquestionably, the most important thing you're being informed of *Unconsciously* is what the situation means. And the meaning of any situation causes you to decide and behave accordingly.

Three different people could get pulled over by the police for speeding. One person might suddenly drive off in a panic and get chased and arrested for resisting the law; the second person might sit sullenly while the cops write them a ticket; the third driver might engage pleasantly with the police, who respond in kind and send them off with a warning. Of course, there could be many different variables at play in each scenario, but for illustration's sake, let's just say that the conditions are exactly the same in each situation.

The first person's *Ego* makes sense of the situation by checking with their *Belief System*, which holds a self-definition of "I am bad," a definition of authority as abusive, and a definition of the world as a dangerously volatile environment. Based on that *Unconscious* set of definitions, this individual's sense of what will likely happen next is that they will be persecuted, and the same thoughts and feelings that tell them that also urgently propose they flee the scene.

The second person's *Ego* has a less disturbing take of the situation, but nevertheless one that still positions them as a powerless player. Their unconscious definitions of self, others, and the world are that they themselves are powerless, authority is overwhelmingly powerful, and the world is unfair. They feel that punishment is inevitable and there is nothing they can do about it, other than glower silently to show their dissatisfaction with the rules of life.

The third person, meanwhile, has a completely positive relationship to the same event. Just like the other two, their *Ego* establishes "how it is" here by checking in with their *Belief System*, but comes up with a completely different set of assumptions than the others did. Their *Unconscious* definition of self is that they are likable when at a disadvantage, authority is a tolerant force, and the world is a benign environment. As the policeman approaches, ticket book in hand, this driver feels a sense of elation; they are stirred to greet the officer cheerfully, and happily acknowledge their error. The person's disarming disposition wears down the policeman's resolve to punish them, and the cop lets them off with a polite reminder of the dangers of breaking the speed limit.

The above permutations of *Unconscious* definitions can't be found in any textbook. They vary significantly from individual to individual, accounting for the uniqueness of our personalities. They do, however, serve to illustrate how we form our perceptions and how those perceptions drive our behavior and, ultimately, how we create a life condition resembling our beliefs.

You've most probably heard the adage, "In politics, perception is reality." Or "In advertising, perception is reality." Or "In Hollywood, perception is reality." The saying is used to suggest that a certain section of society is especially out of touch with reality. It implies that perception is not an accurate reflection of reality, but that in these worlds people act as if it is. It's a marvelous aphorism, conveying so much in so few words, though applicable to all of us, not just the more evidently narcissistic cliques in society.

Perception is not a reflection of objective reality; it is a reflection of the definitions we hold at any time, as communicated to us through our thoughts and feelings. It is so seamlessly built into our *Self Conscious* awareness that questioning it seems absurd. After all, our other senses of sight and hearing and touch and smell and taste appear to be so reliable, why not everything else we apprehend? And that is the advantage our *Ego* has over our *Genius*—our perception is conveyed to us through our senses, and backed up by a solid history of consistent experiences. It makes palpable, tangible sense. Yet, in truth, what we think and feel is going on is a very limited and distorted view of what *actually* is going on.

Later, when we cover personality types, I'm going to go into the various creatively counterproductive worldviews we get sucked into by our perceptions. For now, let's agree that if they are based on our *Unconscious Beliefs*, they will tend to be colored by our psychological wounds and offer a *Low-Level Creative Perspective* and life orientation. Here I just want to look at how we can neutralize our (creatively low-level) *Perception* and shift into a *High-Level Creative Perspective*. How do we prepare the fertile grounds for our *Genius* to emerge? The answer is surprisingly simple.

First, we must go back to asking ourselves, "How is our *Low-Level Creative Perception* formed?" The answer, of course, is that in needing to know "how it is"—in needing to understand and have everything worked out—the *Ego* dips into our *Unconscious Beliefs* and then dredges up our predetermined definitions and assumptions and theories relating to our present situation, and communicates all of that to us through our thoughts and feelings. Our sense of the now is based more on memory than a direct apprehension of current reality. *It's inescapable that* Perception *will be our inevitable mode of awareness as long as we need to know "how it is."*

So, the next question, then, is, "How can we neutralize our *Perception* and shift into a *Genius* state of consciousness, where our whole experience of reality is born of a refreshed and inspired relationship to the moment, rather than informed by what we made up in infancy and early childhood?" And the answer, quite obviously, is...don't know how it is! Let go of your need to understand and work everything out. Stop assuming that you have the answers or even need them. Stop making sense.

IN NO SENSE

When you consciously suspend your *Unconscious* need to know, you enter into a state of *Innocence*. I like to refer to it as *In No Sense*—a place outside of thoughts and feelings. *Innocence* is a state of awe and wonder in which everything is either encountered for the first time or where awareness is not influenced by prior experience. This quality is what Jimi Hendrix was referring to in a *Life* magazine interview: "A musician, if he's a messenger, is like a child who hasn't been handled too many times by man, hasn't had too many fingerprints across his brain."[2]

In the early nineteen-nineties I was living in the inner Sydney suburb of Balmain, when it was transforming from an industrial dockland into a chic harborside residential area. One blustery winter's day I was walking along the

---

2 Jimi Hendrix, interviewed in Robin Richman, "An Infinity of Jims," Life Magazine, October 3, 1969, p. 74.

waterfront, chewing over a multitude of challenges confronting my life. The surroundings did nothing to uplift me. It was a time when global environmental consciousness was at its peak, and I couldn't help but feel disheartened by the signs of past and present ecological recklessness all around me. A row of dilapidated warehouses and factory buildings with stained walls and broken windows and crumbling smokestacks stood forlornly on the other side of the narrow bay. Rusty steel pipes cantilevered out over the bilgy water, evoking visions of toxic waste discharging wholesale into the harbor. Down at water level the tide had receded, exposing grimy sand beaches covered in oil slicks. Jagged pieces of beer-bottle glass were strewn across the sand, thanks to the mindless drunks who staggered down from the pub on the hill after closing time. Huge splotches of seagull shit adorned the sandstone promenade, while the culprits themselves perched morosely along the wharf railings bracing themselves against the chill wind. The smell of shit and floating detritus and diesel fumes from boats idling on their moorings turned my stomach with every fresh gust.

My only consolation was the solitude afforded by the grim weather, but even that was ruined by a noisy mob of pre-school-aged children running towards me in advance of a young mother pushing a pram. She had a look of grim stoicism on her face that broadcasted her clear resolve to be unaffected by anything whatsoever, pleasant or unpleasant. To my horror, and the mother's indifference, the kids bolted down a set of slimy sandstone steps onto the tarred beach below me. I winced at the thought of how dirty and dangerous it was down there with all the oil and broken glass. Simultaneously, I felt a surge of pity for these suburban urchins forced to play in such an unnatural and polluted environment.

The kids didn't care at all, though. As far as they were concerned they were in wonderland. "Wow!" they squealed, pointing to the oil slicks. "Look, Mum, can you see the rainbows all over the sand down here?" Everything was amazing to them. Their eyes did not overlook a single detail of their surroundings, and all they saw impressed them: bits of cyan and cobalt plastic, little crabs with eyes on stalks, bait fish shoaling in the shallows—even the broken glass. They held pieces of beer bottle up to the feeble sun, angling the glass fragments to achieve a prism effect, and then cried out in fresh wonder, "Wow! Look at the colors. Look at the colors."

It struck me in that moment how distorted my outlook on life was. Here I was, immersed in the wonder of existence, standing at the center of an extraordinarily multifarious universe, surrounded by a vast variety of life forms and the manifestations of mind-boggling creativity, both human and Divine. Clouds were forming and dissolving, birds were taking flight and landing, voices rose loudly and then fell silent. The skies—the moment—my mind—everything was pregnant with possibility. Anything could have been born in that instant. But there I was locked into my preconceived notion that life was hard, that winter was miserable, that the planet was choking to death, that humans were a blight on the landscape. In other words, I was weighed down by what I brought to that situation, not by the situation itself.

Joseph Campbell, the mythology guru, made the observation that the mind catalogues information for convenience. It's a dynamic that we should be thankful for. To have to relearn the meaning of all things in our environment every time we encounter them would be a massive waste of energy, not to mention be life-threatening. When I'm back in Africa, for instance, walking along a path in the bush, it's handy that I already have my surroundings figured out. I won't startle in fright at the warble of a thrush in the undergrowth, and I won't hang around to get bitten by an angry snake as that loud rustling in the tall grass moves inexorably towards me.

There are some obvious drawbacks to this cataloguing function, of course. Qualitatively, it makes us stale and depressed. Every day new blossoms bloom in our gardens but we don't appreciate them fully because our rational minds assume, *Unconsciously*, that we know all there is to know about flowers. We hug our loved ones but the warmth of that connection won't sink in too deep because, again, we figure we don't have anything more to learn about these existing connections. Rationally we don't want to fully absorb any experience we assume won't teach us anything new. We perceive things vaguely, not in any detail, because the details supposedly already exist in our catalogue. So our experiences and relationship to people and things become very shallow, very bland—which then causes us to dry up inside. We no longer have a vital, living, breathing connection to life, but instead live out of a suitcase of musty experiences we packed many years ago.

Creatively, the uninterrupted reference we make to our *Unconscious* catalogue keeps us oblivious to our *Genius* perspective and input. By not needing to be fully present, we are not aware of the deeper levels of reality in our field of *Self Conscious* awareness. We filter out a swathe of objective details that are relevant to us in the moment. Whether it be visual imagery or mental ideas or a certain sense of something, that which is so obviously standing out begging to be realized is pushed back into the dim recesses of awareness in favor of a convenient, preconceived summary of current reality. What would truly serve us to be aware of, what might be in our greater interest to be involved in, what could be more pleasing or effective, escapes us.

The perversity of a total capitulation to our rational cataloguing function is beautifully summed up by author Bob Samples who, when presenting his interpretation of Einstein's perspective on intuition, wrote: "Albert Einstein called the intuitive or metaphoric mind a sacred gift. He added that the rational mind was a faithful servant. It is paradoxical that in the context of modern life we have begun to worship the servant and defile the divine."[3] I am no religious scholar, but in the King James Bible when Jesus is tempted by the Devil, he says, "Get thee behind me, Satan." Metaphorically, he might well be commanding his *Uncon-*

---

3 Bob Samples, The Metaphoric Mind: A Celebration Of Creative Consciousness (Reading, Massachusettes: Addison-Wesley Publishing Co., Inc., 1976), p. 26.

scious catalogue to stand back in order to allow his *Super Conscious* input to move to the forefront of his awareness.

We can very easily put the faithful servant back in his place, and get Satan to get himself behind us. All we have to do is suspend our need to be in the know. When we do that, when we allow ourselves to be in the mystery, we cut ourselves off from our rote catalogue, and we are suddenly more fully connected to our current reality. We go into *In No Sense*.

The condition of *Innocence* can be described as a refreshed, heightened state of appreciation. Everything seems to stand out, become more vivid and alive. Our immediate and intimate connection to whatever we behold gives it a wondrous quality. Beauty is bestowed on our world by the novel and unique light we see it in. Time apparently stands still as our senses soak up the marvelous details of our experience—just as it did for those kids playing on the polluted beach, while their mother and I grappled unhappily with the problematic definitions and meaning served up by our well-thumbed catalogues.

Innocence is definitely a childlike condition. But don't for a moment confuse it with childish naivety or ignorance. Wise men and women throughout history have revered *Innocence* as the basis of our creative power. You'll find references to it everywhere: in religious texts, Alchemical principles, the verses of the Romantic Poets, the Grail myth, and even in our modern-day mythology. In the epic sci-fi movie *Star Wars*, when the young hero, Luke Skywalker, is making his final do-or-die bombing run over the evil Empire's Death Star, he hears the voice of his mentor Obi-Wan Kenobi's spirit urging him to "Use the Force, Luke. Let go, Luke."[4] Luke shuts down his star fighter's onboard computer system and syncs his mind with the mystical Universal Force, which then guides him to fly and target the Death Star instinctively. If ever there was a nod to the premise of shifting from the mechanically driven mode of

---

4   Star Wars: Episode IV – A New Hope, Film, written and directed by George Lucas (George Lucas and 20th Century Fox, 1977).

Perception to the mystically connected mode of *Intuition*, this is it. By suspending his reliance on his preprogrammed rational intelligence system, Luke prepares his mind to receive the inspired direction of his own *Genius*. So too for us, *In No Sense* is the bridge to our *Intuition*.

(For an audio of an *In No Sense* guided meditation, please go to williamwhitecloud.com/naturalsuccessbonus/.

RECEIVING

Probably the most revered character in Japanese history is the legendary seventeenth-century swordsman Shinmen Takezo, better known as Miyamoto Musashi. His fighting ability was on a par with that of his French counterpart, Cyrano de Bergerac, though while de Bergerac's exploits are mostly fictional, Musashi's were mostly for real. He is said to have single-handedly taken on a hundred men at a time and killed them all. His prowess owed to a phenomenal *Natural Ability*, ferocious focus, and a complete reliance on instinct over technique. In *The Book of Five Rings*, which he wrote in retirement, Musashi repeatedly remarks that technical flourishes are excessive, and drives home the principle that technique has less value than focusing on the end result of cutting down one's opponent. I don't recall too many specifics from the book other than the chilling advice that the best way to unnerve your opponent is by stabbing straight at his face.

Musashi's career ran concurrently with that of another great swordsman, the dashing Sasaki Kojiro, who went by the fighting name of Ganryu. Unlike Musashi, Ganryu was a big fan of technique. He was the arch exponent of the *kenjutsu* style of sword fighting, using a long two-handed sword and dispatching his opponents with a move he had perfected by cutting down flying swallows. Like Musashi, Ganryu had triumphed in many epic duels, and there was great debate and speculation in the whole of Japan as to which of them was the supreme fighter, though the odds favored Ganryu because of his long-blade advantage.

In a world where no warrior's reputation went unchallenged, it was inevitable that the two greatest swordsmen of their time would have to face each other sooner or later, and so it came to pass that a duel between them was arranged. A date was set for the 13th of April, 1612, and the rules of engagement were carefully negotiated. To avoid any treachery by the competing teams, it was decided that they would fight it out on a small island in the middle of a lake where there could be no surprise attacks by either of the combatant's henchmen. Both swordsmen would be rowed out to the island, where they would be left to do battle on their own. The rules provided for the duelists to go out separately the day before to look the island over. Ganryu took advantage of the opportunity to familiarize himself with the terrain. Musashi demurred, saying that he did not want to go into the fight with any preconceived notions whatsoever.

The duel between Ganryu and Musashi was one of the greatest spectacles in Samurai history. A grandstand was built around the lake to accommodate the hordes of spectators coming to witness this fight to the death between two living legends. At the appointed time on the appointed day, Ganryu was ferried out to the little island, from where he acknowledged the cheers of the excited crowd. Musashi, meanwhile, was nowhere to be seen. Hours passed and still he did not show up. Ganryu paced the spit of earth in rage. Speculation was rife among the spectators that Musashi had chickened out for fear of having no answer to his opponent's long, two-handed sword. By the time the sun began its descent into the western sky and it was starting to register with onlookers that there would be no fight, people began to allow that they had never believed Musashi was any match for Ganryu, anyway, and weren't surprised that when it came down to it, he had run away with his tail between his legs.

Some three hours after his nemesis had set out from the lakeshore to the island, Musashi finally deigned to turn up. No student of the famous duel is in doubt that his tardiness was entirely calculated to rile Ganryu. After all, his whole aim in every conflict was to remain still and centered within himself, and at the same time spook his opponents into reaction. Even so, as he climbed into the rowing boat that would transport him to his waiting adversary, Musashi was nursing concerns about how he might overcome Ganryu's long-blade advantage. How would he get close enough to his opponent without being taken out by the fabled "turning swallow" cut?

The boatman took up his oars and began rowing the boat in the direction of the island. A jeer went up in the stands, partly as a rebuke to Musashi for his blatant disrespect, but also in elated anticipation of the epic duel the crowd was finally on the verge of witnessing. After all, this was "Rumble in the Jungle" medieval-Japan style. The great swordsman ignored the jeers and concentrated instead on calming his mind. As he did so, the thing that came to his attention was that there was a spare oar in the boat—a long, slender pole with a paddle blade at one end—longer than Ganryu's *no-dachi* sword! Without hesitating, Musashi took out his own sword and began whittling away at the pole, chopping off the paddle blade and, as best he could, fashioning the oar into the semblance of a blunt, wooden sword.

When Musashi reached the island, Ganryu stood seething next to the waterline with the sinking sun in his eyes. The kenjutsu master watched Musashi get out of the boat holding an oar. He drew his sword from its scabbard and threw the scabbard aside with a curse. In that moment Musashi had his rival at a complete disadvantage: Ganryu was hopping mad, he had the sun in his eyes, and he was expecting Musashi to put the oar down and draw his own sword. Instead, from out of reach of the long blade, Musashi swung his crude oar "sword" with all his might, landing a blow on Ganryu's side, which crushed his pelvis. Ganryu went down in a heap. Musashi took a step forward and caved in his fallen opponent's head with another swing of the oar "sword." Musashi walked back to the boat that had brought him and was about to climb in. As an afterthought, he turned and bowed to Ganryu's prone body and then climbed into the boat, nodding to the boatman to row him back to the mainland. It was Musashi's last fight ever. And Ganryu's.

We don't hear about this story much in relation to

Creative or Intuitive Development, although we should. In the same way that Wag Dodge was able to make a creative leap of incredible magnitude when he took an instinctive stand against the reactive compulsions of his emotions, Musashi was able to consistently operate on a *High-Level Creative Frequency* by being so fiercely disciplined in not allowing himself to be influenced by preconceived strategies, techniques, or theories and concepts. As a result of his value of living in *In No Sense*, Musashi always had the advantage of recognizing the most effective pathway in any undertaking, as well as the ability to have his *Natural Ability* bring things together in a way he could never have engineered rationally or *Self Consciously*. The legendary swordsman's *Genius*, like most real *Genius*, was not a function of brilliant deductive reasoning, but rather the opposite—an ability to let go of working everything out and, from there, recognizing *Super Conscious* input as it arose. This is, in fact, the creative principle of *Receiving*.

Receiving is one of the most important aspects of *High-Level Creative Function*, something we can only embody when we let go of needing to have everything worked out. Often enough I've heard the saying, "Let go and let God," and I'm not sure whether those who utter the phrase know how profound it actually is. Wise people as diverse as Albert Einstein and Joseph Campbell tell us that our rational brain is really a secondary organ designed for objective analysis. As marvelous as it is at that function, we know it has the drawback of working with a set of information that is limited by the extent of our linear experience and the scope of our biases. In the 2004 quantum physics documentary/feature film *What the Bleep Do We Know!?*, one of the featured experts, Dr. Joe Dispenza, claims that the human brain processes *four hundred billion* bits of information every second, while we are only *Self Consciously* aware of *two thousand* bits. That's a massive discrepancy! Just like a judge rules at the beginning of a trial what evidence can and cannot be used in the court case, so there must be some part of our brain deciding what of all eternity we should be allowed to see at any time. And I'm betting that it's the same two thousand bits that we always see—those that fit in with and make sense of what we already know about "how it is" from before.

Rationally, we don't stand much chance of coming up with anything different than our *Unconscious Beliefs* of "how it is." That transcendent function belongs to the *Super Conscious* mind, the part of us connected to, and capable of processing, everything through all time and space. Yet in our society, as Bob Samples said, the rational mind has usurped the role of the *Super Conscious*. We tend to live our lives by trying to work them out, never realizing why we might be so stuck in such an unsatisfying experience of our careers, or lifestyles, or relationships, or social involvement, or health, or creative expression. The harder people try to give up their addictions, or overcome their financial problems, or hang on to their relationships, or control their lives, the more their problems seem to compound. Which is why every time someone just "lets go and lets God," it's such an incredibly liberating feeling, and so often leads to the person creating a better situation for themselves.

There is a commonly accepted saying: "No problem can be solved by the same kind of thinking that created it." When anyone gives up trying to hold their life together, they are inevitably giving up rational control, which suspends their *Unconscious* referencing and allows their *Natural Ability* some room to move. No offense to anyone's religious beliefs, but what may seem like the miraculous hand of God taking over is likely to be the person's own *Genius* filling the breach. Generally it's true that the less we insist on how we assume things have to be, the more brilliantly our lives tend to flow. Have you heard that great saying, "Would you rather be right or happy?"[5]

On a trip I recently took back to Australia, a friend of mine reminded me of the phenomenally successful business he created using the tools he had learnt from me in my

---

5 Helen Schucman, scribe, A Course In Miracles, vol. 1 (Temecula, Calif.: Foundation For Inner Peace, 1976).

first-generation training, "Living from Greatness," way back at the end of the nineties, most specifically the principle of *Receiving*. Fergus Herbert certainly fits the description *maverick entrepreneur*. Fergus has made his fortune by getting involved in the most unlikely ventures ranging from publishing, to buying a gold mine, to owning Jatropha plantations, to developing unconventional properties, to aqua farming.

Around the time of the terrorist attack on the Twin Towers in New York, Fergus was running a disruptive valve technology company from his offices in the iconic Sydney landmark the Manly Bathers Pavilion, which he had just bought and was in the process of redeveloping. One day he got a call from an MBA graduate who had interned for him at Global Valve Technology. The young man wasn't happy with his current employment situation and wanted to know if Fergus knew of any good positions available in the management world. Fergus told him in his genial way that he didn't, but he'd let him know if something came up.

Just minutes after he hung up on his former intern, the phone rang again. This time it was a friend of his who was about to lose his job selling advertising. He too was wondering if Fergus knew of any work in his area of expertise. As with the intern, he had to tell his friend that he didn't, but he'd let him know if something came up.

Fergus remembers thinking what a coincidence it was being called minutes apart by two highly competent executives looking for work. But that isn't where it ended. A little while later his phone rang again. Incredibly, it was another friend calling to find out if Fergus knew anyone who needed any graphic design work done, because things were pretty desperate in his field at the time. He had to tell the graphic designer exactly what he had told the last two callers.

From everything I know about Fergus, he's an affable guy, as well as highly pragmatic. While on the one hand he really wished he could do something for his friends, he also regretted seeing so much talent going to waste. Before the end of the day an idea came to him and he called back all three men and invited them to a meeting at his office the following day, hinting that he might have some work for them.

When they turned up for the meeting at the Bathers Pavilion, each of them was equally surprised to learn that it was not a private meeting with Fergus. Their suspicion and disappointment were soon allayed, however, when he told them that he had an idea for a business that would involve each of their diverse talents.

"Oh, great!" they all chimed excitedly. "What is it?"

"Well, that's the thing," Fergus said with a rakish grin and raised finger. The trio sat forward in their seats. "I don't know."

The three men looked around at each other, confounded. "But you just told us you had an idea for a business that could use all of our talents," his would-be partners balked. "How can we go into business if you haven't even got one in mind?"

"Well, that's the thing," Fergus explained, "we're going to find a business."

"Are you nuts, mate?" one of the others exclaimed. "This isn't the right time in the economic cycle to be starting a business."

Another put up his hands and said flatly, "I haven't got any money to put into a business. I'm out."

"How will we ever find a business that suits all four of us?" the third one frowned.

After withstanding a tirade of doubts and objections, Fergus put his idea to his friends. "Here's the plan. We go into business as equal partners. We'll give it one month to find exactly the right business for all of us. I don't know how we'll find it. We're not going to try to work it out. We're going to hang with the tension until it comes to us, and when it does we'll know it when we see it."

If anyone other than Fergus had put this plan to them, the three men would have walked out there and then. But because of his track record of putting successful deals together in the most unorthodox ways, they were at least disposed to considering his proposal. Now that he had them interested, Fergus made them an offer none of them could refuse. "I'll put up whatever money is needed, and I'll pay your salaries for a year as a loan."

They were all in. Their first order of business was to form a company called Knights of the Round Table, and next they set up a temporary office in the Bathers Pavilion. Enthusiasm was running high. Of course, none of them had any experience with waiting, and every day found one or more of the partners coming to work with some venture for the others to consider. Fergus watched with a detached amusement as the usual suspects of fast food franchises, investment schemes, bankruptcy notifications, and hot tips were paraded through the boardroom. Everyone was doing their heads in trying to force a suitable opportunity through the one-month window Fergus had set. The walls of their office were plastered with flip chart sheets cataloguing the business models and numbers relating to all the schemes they were coming up with. But nothing anyone brought in managed to excite a majority of the shareholders. Every time one of his partners asked him in exasperation how they were going to find the right business, Fergus had the same answer, "I don't know."

As the deadline approached, everyone's enthusiasm began turning to despair. They consoled themselves and each other with the fact that they had lost nothing more than a few weeks of their time. Though they were all disappointed, no one harbored any hard feelings. With a week still left to the agreed deadline, the partners started thinking about looking for work outside of the Round Table again.

Two days before the month was up, the graphic designer came to Fergus desperate for some work. He asked Fergus to think of anyone he could approach who might be able to give him a lead. Fergus suggested he talk to an acquaintance of his, Gill, who had some publishing interests. The designer went to see Gill the same day, and came back to the office just before the close of business to collect his personal effects. He didn't expect he'd ever be coming back.

"So, did he have anything for you?" Fergus said when he saw the designer.

"No," the man replied dejectedly, "but he asked if you can go see him."

Seeing as though Gill's offices were nearby to his own, Fergus decided to drop in on him first thing the following morning. As he walked into Gill's office, the businessman dispensed with all pleasantries and asked Fergus bluntly, "Have you got two dollars in your pocket?"

"I think so," said Fergus, taken aback. "Why, do you want me to go grab you a coffee?"

"No," Gill waived the suggestion away. "It's what I want for two of my magazines."

Turned out that Gill had two magazines—a regional airline's inflight magazine and a cruise line's journal—that he was losing money publishing. He proposed Fergus take them off him in return for two dollars and fifty percent of future profits. Fergus, having cut his teeth in the early days as a publisher, instinctively knew he had found the unicorn he and his friends were looking for. It had, as he said it would, come to him—on the last day of the deadline, too. Just as Musashi had, he took decisive action. Without bothering to look at any numbers, he countered with an offer of two dollars and six and a half percent of Knights of the Round Table. Gill accepted.

As soon as he got back to the Bathers Pavilion, Fergus summoned his partners. "Okay, lads," he told them once they had all gathered, "we're in business. Here's the deal. The inflight magazine goes to press later today. We have advertising sales of twenty thousand dollars and production costs of twenty-five thousand. We've got a few hours to get costs down and sell more advertising."

The advertising executive worked the phones that day and brought in two thousand dollars in advertising. By the time the magazine went to press, Fergus had found a way to cut production costs by five thousand dollars. They had just bought a business for two dollars and in four hours made a profit of two thousand dollars. From there they took the inflight magazine from a quarterly to a monthly publication. Not only that, they began acquiring other airlines' inflight magazines.

Soon they were doing so well that they were able to buy another iconic landmark in Manly, a former Masonic Lodge known as The Temple, for just under two million dollars. If you are familiar with the esoteric origins of the Freemasons, you will appreciate the delicious irony of this acquisition.

Once the Knights of the Round Table set up office in The Temple, they began expanding their media business even further. The centerpiece of their enterprise was a digital agency called Edge, which was named by *Business Review Weekly* as Australia's fastest-growing company many years in a row. Within a decade The Temple was home to seventy employees and operations turning over twenty million dollars annually.

The story doesn't end there. Leveraging their success with the original business, the individual partners were able to create other lucrative projects reflecting their own private interests and expertise. Most notable of these is King Content, a content marketing agency, which ultimately sold for a staggering amount of money that I am not at liberty to disclose.

And herein, folks, is a case study in magic, especially relating to the principle of *Receiving*. Though, I must say, this story is a gift that keeps on giving. I will make reference to it in the next two chapters, *Following Through* and *Using the Emotion of the True End Result*. But for now, let me just reiterate: when we operate on a *High-Level Creative Frequency*, we harmonize with the miraculous nature of existence and bring into being extraordinary creations that defy our expectations of what is possible, and simultaneously enrich ourselves and all that we are a part of. Applying his own *Genius*, Fergus not only made a ton of money, he also created opportunities for an untold number of others, and even beyond that, generated the resources to invest in many socially uplifting and environmentally sustainable projects. It really is a beautiful thing.

OBSERVING THE OBVIOUS

As you can see from the Musashi myth and the example of my talented business friend Fergus, *In No Sense* should not be associated with childish naivety and ignorance. Operating in a way where we have loosened our grip on needing to understand and have everything worked out can, and should be, applied to military strategy, business development, sports performance, artistic endeavor, learning, innovation, scientific research, leadership, conflict resolution, relationships, quality of life, and absolutely any and every area of human interest or activity. But it's not as easy as it sounds. The thing that Musashi and Fergus have in common is that they had both intentionally developed their mode of awareness known as *Intuition*, and you'll need to develop and practice your *Intuition* if you mean to apply it in any consistent and masterful way.

I don't mean to be arrogant, but I do laugh when I read scholarly articles on intuition and the authors still frame it in terms of a sixth sense, hunches, and gut feelings, as though it's a vague and intermittent dynamic that visits us at its own pleasure or whim. That's like saying that no matter how well you learn to speak Portuguese, and you travel to Brazil, you'll only be able to catch snatches of what the locals are saying on random occasions, rather than have fluent conversations the whole time. Please! *Intuition* is one of our primary modes of awareness, constantly available and accessible at will. Though, I must say, to begin with, your rational mind will be a lot happier about you learning Portuguese than it will be about coexisting with your *Intuition*.

Perhaps if I give you a dictionary definition of *Intuition* you will understand the challenge one faces in being able to master it: *What the mind immediately apprehends before rationalizing*. Do you see the problem? In going into *In No Sense*, information that doesn't normally occur to you suddenly stands out. Super-rational knowing can come in many different forms: the clichéd gut feeling or funny sense of something, vague impressions, obvious knowing, symbolic association, imagery, colors or lights, physical sensations. There is no limit to the variety of ways in which *Genius* insight and inspiration show up. It is neither possible nor necessary to have a catalogue of every potential cognitive vessel the information will be contained in. If you are trained in *Intuition*, you will recognize and allow yourself to receive any sign of latent wisdom the moment you become aware of it. If you are untrained, you will *Self Consciously* do what you are always *Unconsciously* doing—wipe your mind clear of anything that doesn't make sense to your rational mind. In other words, though an infinite quantity of information is dawning on you, you will continue to rationalize everything to fit in with what you know from the past. Your rational mind makes sure that nothing more than your preselected, preapproved two thousand bits survive the light of *Self Conscious* awareness.

A friend of mine once told me an interesting story related to this dynamic. When he was a boy, he lived with his family in South Australia in an area known for its high level of UFO activity. One clear sunny day he was driving back home from somewhere with his father, when they both witnessed a formation of lights come flying at them head-on and then veer off the highway and disappear into the sky just in time to avoid collision. Both he and his father were shaken by the experience. After all, something of an otherworldly nature travelling at lightning speed had nearly crashed into them.

At first, my friend recounted, he and his dad were incredulous. They did that thing we all do when startled: "Did you see that?"

"Yes, did you see that?"

"Yes, what was that?"

"I don't know. Do you know? What do you think?"

After the initial shock wore off they both felt elated at the shared experience of a close encounter with an evidently extraterrestrial object. Both father and son used the term *UFO* in referring to what they had just seen. Soon my friend's father's common sense kicked in. "Well," he said, "we don't know what it was. It could have been anything. Could have been foo fighters, those orbs of light that followed bomber planes at high altitudes in the war. Or balloons. Whatever it was, it was very strange. Gave us a good fright, hey son?" They ended up agreeing that whatever it was they had seen, there had to be some logical, non-phenomenological explanation for it, although they still agreed that it had been an incredible experience.

But when they got home, and my friend ran inside to tell the rest of the family what had happened to them on the road, his father refused to back up his story. He denied point-blank that they had seen anything at all, never mind anything out of the ordinary. Even years later, when my friend asked his father in private why he had denied the mysterious experience, his old man refused to acknowledge that something had happened and dismissed his son's memory of the incident as the product of an overactive imagination.

That's a cruel thing to happen to a boy. Why my friend's father didn't back him up isn't something I can definitively explain, but his denial of the incident serves to illustrate perfectly how the rational mind whittles down reality to fit it in with its preconceived notion of "how it is." First something comes into awareness—it is objectively apprehended by the mind—and then the process of rationalization begins. While usually this editing is happening at the blink of an eye, the father's repression mechanism can be seen here in slow motion.

To begin with, the mind recognizes the object just for what it is. As originally noted, the father and son referred openly to what they had seen as a UFO. Next, the mind tries to square the object with what it knows from before. The father began to explain the phenomenon in terms of what in his linear experience could have caused it—foo fighters or balloons floating on the highway. If the object can fit in with the mind's worldview, then it will survive in *Self Conscious* awareness, albeit in the subjective context it has been squeezed into. If it doesn't fit in with the mind's worldview, it is wiped clean from *Self Conscious* awareness.

What is interesting is that the father could fit the experience into the framework of his past understanding—foo fighters, balloons, light reflecting off something on the Nullarbor Plain, perhaps. Considering that his son also saw something, it's feasible that a weird incident of some kind did actually occur. Yet the father ended up denying the entire experience, and apparently not just in the sense that he simply refused to admit it, but in that he ended up truly having no recollection of it. In that case, another kind of rationalizing influence is likely at work—*Conforming Tendency*.

In their book on institutional change, *Presence*, authors Betty Sue Flowers, Joseph Jaworski, Otto Scharmer, and Peter Senge point out that further than our minds needing to establish "how it is" individually, we also have a fundamental social need to agree on "how it is." All young children are aware of otherworldly beings like fairies and pixies. They all see angels above their beds or little green men at the window. In many cultures, even today, these daemonic entities—considered intermediaries between the physical and metaphysical planes—are commonly accepted as normal. But as children grow up in our society, they fall into agreement with the adults whom they are catching up with that there are no such things, to the point that they forget they ever saw them. If my friend and his father belonged to a skeptical social group who strongly refuted the validity of any type of phenomenon, then I can understand how the father's *Conforming Tendency* was the final determinant in banishing the close encounter he had with a UFO from his *Self Conscious* reality altogether.

This is one of the challenges you will face trying to apply your *Intuition*. You may well go into *In No Sense* and suddenly become aware of a whole lot of new information, but if that information does not fit in with what you have psychically agreed on with your peer group, or match your sense of self, or others, or the world, or possibility, or if you didn't come by the information through a linear process such as a chain of events or hearing it from someone else, or if it contradicts conventional wisdom or the face value of anything, you are going to throw those realizations under the bus of rationalization quicker than you can count to one.

The rational mind, I must warn you, is a fierce guardian of its domain. It jealously serves the *Ego* in keeping you orientated—holding you to a perception consistent with your beliefs about "how it is." If you ever begin entertaining input from outside its purview, the rational mind will use extreme methods, if necessary, to make sure you let the foreign impressions go. Normally you won't even notice the shame or doubt or anxiety or depression or sense of emptiness arising as new realities dawn on you, because you tend to dismiss those realities before they ever occur to you in *Self Conscious* awareness. But you can be sure you will notice the tension as soon as you do become cognizant of nonsensical realities, and you can rely on the tension ratcheting up to unbearable levels the longer you sit with the "nonsense."

In *The Search for the Real Self*, psychiatrist James Masterson, M.D., refers to this kind of pain as "abandonment depression." He doesn't mean depression in the strict sense of the word, using the term to include all negative emotions that arise when we begin to stray from and ignore our conditioned sense of self. The mystic George Gurdjieff, who influenced modern psychology with his concepts of higher consciousness, saw these tensions as "buffers" that cushion us from the psychological turmoil that ensues when our identity is challenged. Mythology also has a lot to say about our psychological reluctance to embrace whatever lies further afield of our certainly established world. Anyone who is familiar with the work of J.R.R. Tolkien knows that hobbits are not allowed to leave the cozy, pleasant climes of their beloved Shire. Terror lives beyond its borders. And Tolkien tells us plainly what that terror is when he describes hobbits as little people who love to read books full of things they already know about.

I don't want to give the rational mind the power. Your *Creative Spirit* is infinitely more powerful. Nevertheless, psychological resistance to the *new* is a fact of life that is best faced rather than swept under the carpet. Living life on a *High-Level Creative Frequency* is a freedom you have to fight for. This is what it means to be a *Creative Warrior*. It takes a fierce dedication to just *notice reality without jumping to what it means*. This is a skill I call, quite literally, *Observing the Obvious*.

People use the word *obvious* all the time, though few are ever really functionally aware of it. The obvious is what plainly jumps out at you and stays with you in objective form. Great power will come to anyone who can learn to be present to whatever is, without needing to understand what they apprehend, no matter how perplexing or confronting. I guarantee that the ability to *Observe the Obvious* will improve your powers of creative awareness a hundred times! When I teach *Intuition*, just about the most powerful technique I introduce my participants to is one where they observe someone talking, with all their senses paying attention, and then just feed back exactly what jumped out at them, no matter how absurd they perceive their observations to be. What my pupils learn is that if they can be true to themselves, regardless of their discomfort, they can access insights so deep, so apparently "hidden," that one would consider them to be highly gifted psychics.

***

So, to recap, here's what we have established about applying *Intuition* so far: In order for us to prepare the fertile grounds for our *Genius* to emerge, we suspend our need to understand and know "how it is"—we go into *In No Sense*. Once we are in *In No Sense*, we experience a heightened sense of awareness that allows in information from beyond our routine perceptions. When we hold with this new information, we awaken to inspired input served up by the *Unlimited Self* we sometimes refer to as the *Soul*. We make connections between things that haven't been made before, on levels we haven't reached before. If we are lovers, we realize a passion beyond words; if we are songwriters, we hear sublime melodies; if we are poets, the Muse gifts us words to soar on; if we are leaders, we keep open the heart of our collective undertakings; if we are entrepreneurs, we see needs in the marketplace and approaches to our customers that blow away existing models; if we are inventors, the secrets of the universe reveal themselves to us; if we are travellers, we leave our own world behind us and truly appreciate the spice of adventure in other worlds.

Yet, all the time, inevitably, *Emotional Tension* arises afresh to persuade us that our *Creative* awareness is wrong, that it will lead us astray, hurt us, humiliate us. When that happens, there are two principles that we must bear in mind, that will not only help us stay present to our *Genius* input, but will actually enhance the power of our intuitive process.

Firstly, any time tension brews in relation to some awareness we are considering, it's caused by the rational mind grappling with that reality, because we have inadvertently slipped back into trying to comprehend reality rather than just being with it. Losing focus is only human, and it happens to the most masterful among us. When it comes to *Intuition*, mastery is not defined by your ability to never lose focus but by your ability to refocus. If we switch off the rationalizing autopilot again by going back into *In No Sense*, the tension will relax and our intuitive awareness will amplify.

One of the greatest *Genius*-crushing misconceptions we inherit in our society is that we are supposed to navigate life by working it out. *Creative Geniuses* like Musashi know that our *Super Conscious* has it all worked out already, and that the most empowered way to navigate life is receiving the *Obvious*. In this book's final chapter, *Using the Emotion of the True End Result*, we are going to cover *Emotional Tension*—what causes it and how we neutralize it—in more depth, and the principle of refocus will no doubt be more clear and compelling by the time we've finished.

Another creatively destructive misconception we are conditioned to believe is that tension is bad, and something we need to resolve as quickly as possible. Actually tension (as opposed to stress, which we'll also discuss) is the very lifeblood of creativity, and any time we try to eliminate it, we bleed our creative power. Basically, if you can't hang out with tension, you can't create. This is another premise we are going to be looking at in the final chapter—how we use tension to powerfully compel into existence our desired end results. For now, though, I'll just point out that tension is also creative in that it is a psychic accelerant. When we really appreciate this little-known secret, we are more inclined to let go of what we know and lean into any subsequent tension, which has the effect of boosting what we "get" about anything to a breathtaking level.

Intuition is a brilliant mode of awareness—soulful, enchanted and massively empowering. There is nothing that it should not be applied to because there is no circumstance, no matter how sublime or ridiculous, or fantastic or terrible, that cannot benefit considerably from a higher perspective. *In No Sense* is a marvelous bridge to our *Genius* awareness, and *Observing the Obvious* is a powerful technique for apprehending it, but by themselves they do not reveal the full spectrum of our *Super Conscious* knowledge. There is still one more step in fully unpacking our *Intuition*—a step without which the gold of what there is to know will still elude us. You may laugh when you hear what this third phase is, but you will soon stop when you try it on for size. *Making It Up* is everything when it comes to *High-Level Creative Function*.

MAKING IT UP

We all know of multitalented individuals, but it's a rare thing to meet or hear of someone who has variously been a prodigious lover, cleric, army officer, businessman, diplomat, spy, entertainer, magus, politician, con man, writer, and world traveller. The average person is familiar with the name Giacomo Casanova, though most associate him only with his reputation as a legendary seducer and not his many other talents. Without a doubt, he was one of the most flamboyant characters of eighteenth-century Europe, and his varied and colorful exploits make for entertaining reading. My own interest in Casanova, though, is mostly concerned with his leading role in the secret societies of his time. In *The Occult*, possibly the most thorough history of the supernatural you will ever read, Colin Wilson credits Casanova as being one of the three most knowledgeable persons on the subject of magic in the eighteenth century, along with Voltaire and Count Cagliostro, the latter of whom died violently at the hands of the Inquisition. Historically the Catholic Church held a dim view of anything remotely supernatural in nature, and from the fifteenth century right up until the nineteenth century it carried out a formal crusade to eradicate all forms of occult manifestation, considering them to be the Devil's work. Anyone accused of having an interest in or applying any esoteric craft risked the most savage and sadistic punishment imaginable, invariably involving both torture and death.

Casanova was born into a family of commoners in Venice (his mother was the daughter of a cobbler before she eloped with his father, who was an actor from Spain). By all accounts his childhood was not easy. He grew up poor and sickly and suffered from horrible nosebleeds. One time, he had a nosebleed so bad that his grandmother took him to a witch, who locked him in a box while she chanted spells. The bleeding stopped. The witch pulled him from the box and smudged him with the smoke of magic herbs. Finally, she prophesized that he would be visited by a beautiful lady that night. Sure enough, that night Casanova saw a beautiful fairy come out of the fireplace and into his room. The fairy rubbed an ointment on his head and spoke to him in a foreign language. His symptoms vanished, never to return, and he became a healthy and somewhat overconfident boy. Whether or not this account is entirely true, his meeting with the witch was profound enough to confirm for him the powers of the occult.

As a young man, Casanova tried out the usual careers that were in his time considered the most suitable paths of advancement for a gentleman, though neither of his stints as a cleric or an army officer lasted long. He apparently did not have the temperament for structure and discipline. In accordance with his true nature, he ended up in the entertainment business, most notably as "a fiddler for a troupe of daredevils who spent their nights looking for trouble." His fortune, though, soon took a most fortuitous turn when he saved the life of a Venetian senator, who was from the wealthy Bragadin family. The nobleman suffered an apoplectic fit on a gondola, which the young Casanova happened to be sharing. Casanova escorted the gentleman home, where he made the first of the accurate predictions he was to become renowned for throughout the Continent. When he was given leave by the patient's family to go, he famously said, "If I leave, he will die; if I stay, he will get well." And, in fact, if it weren't for Casanova, the aristocrat would likely have passed that night. The attending physician applied a mercury poultice, the cure-all of those days, to his chest. The mercury fumes caused the senator to go into frightening convulsions. It was evident to Casanova that the nobleman was choking to death. Ignoring the protests of the doctor, he washed the mercury off the patient's body and the convulsions soon ended. The nobleman recovered, and was restored to good health as a result of Casanova's prescription of fresh air and a sensible diet.

Being of a cabalistic persuasion, the Bragadin patriarch superstitiously considered Casanova's precocious wisdom to be evidence of a prodigious occult talent, and took the young commoner under his wing, going so far as to treat him as if he were his own son. Taking full advantage of the senator's patronage, Casanova began living the high life. Drawing on a generous allowance, he spent his days and nights partying, womanizing, and gambling, though his activities weren't entirely frivolous—he also dedicated himself to acquiring esoteric knowledge through his benefactor's occult connections.

The good life in Venice wasn't to last for the young romancer, though. Seems he went too far when he dug up a freshly buried corpse to play a joke on an enemy whom he wanted to exact revenge on. The victim of his prank went into paralysis and never recovered. Coming on top of a string of charges concerning him taking liberties with young debutants, it was considered prudent that Casanova take a leave of absence from the city. He wound up in Paris, where, like their relatives all across Europe, the local aristocracy was obsessed with Alchemy. Using his connection to Bragadin, he inveigled his way into the secret societies of the Freemasons and Rosicrucians. Within these occult circles, he met and charmed citizens of high standing. Before long, Casanova was an essential fixture in the parlors of such notable Parisians as Madame de Pompadour, official mistress of King Louis XV; Comte de Saint Germain, another occult initiate; and Jean-Jacques Rousseau, philosopher and author of *The Social Contract*. He delighted his new patrons with his meticulous manners and magical powers, especially his ability to tell fortunes with astonishing accuracy.

Though he clearly possessed a natural occult ability, Casanova always considered himself an imposter. He used his extensive knowledge of the occult mostly to con gullible aristocrats out of sizeable amounts of money. In one case he informed a nobleman that a dagger in the gentleman's collection was the knife Simon Peter used to cut off the ear of Malchus, one of the men who had come to arrest Jesus. He went on to convince the man that if the knife could be restored to its original sheath, then it would give whoever owned it the power to find all of the hidden treasure buried in Christendom. Conveniently he just happened to know where the sheath could be found, and for a sum acquired it for the nobleman. In another instance he performed a ritual intended to transfer the spirit of a grand old dame into the body of a newborn baby so that she could attain immortality. The victims of his scams had no legal recourse because complaining would only have attracted the attention of the Inquisition.

Casanova was equally outrageous in the predictions he made. Called on to tell someone's fortune, he would make up some farfetched prophecy. The interesting thing is, though—and what blew his own mind—was that the prophecies invariably came true. He always followed the same pattern of at first being in awe of his outlandish predictions playing out exactly as he foretold, and then being terrified by his lack of control over the mysterious powers he believed he had loosened. For all his depravity, Casanova was nevertheless a devout Catholic and subject to the superstitions of Christianity that held sway in his lifetime. There were times when he repented his occult ways and went into hiding for fear that God was punishing him for his chicanery by making all his nonsense come true. Casanova's fear was that God would sooner or later visit the same misfortune on him that He was causing in the lives of his clients.

For someone so knowledgeable about the occult, Casanova should have better understood the power of imagination. All throughout history, illuminated individuals of every age have appreciated that we create our own reality and, importantly, credited the imagination with being the miraculous agent enabling that facility. Most probably one esoteric system more than any other has been responsible for championing the imagination from before Plato's time till now, and that is Alchemy. It was practiced in Mesopotamia, Ancient Egypt, Persia, India, Japan, Korea, and China; in Classical Greece and Rome; in the Muslim civilizations; and then in Europe up to the nineteenth century in a complex network of mystery schools and philosophical modalities spanning over two and a half thousand years. In Alchemy, the imagination is referred to cryptically as either "the Philosopher's Stone" or "the Philosopher's Secret Fire"—"a stone that can't be touched" or "a fire that does not burn."

All true students of Alchemy understand the *Genius* of the imagination, its connection to everything through all time and space, and how it can be compelled with the right focus and intention to aid in the creation of wonders. In the West, there was no pre–Industrial Revolution education that was not dripping with Alchemical precepts—most prominently the principles of Neo-platonic and Hermetic philosophy—and its influence and effects can be found in disciplines as disparate as Renaissance art, Romantic poetry, and modern technology and science. No one is surprised to hear names like Leonardo da Vinci or William Blake associated with Alchemy, though many wouldn't ever dream that the man we credit with converting society's imaginative mentality to a mechanical mindset was among the most fervent students of Alchemy of all time. After purchasing and studying Sir Isaac Newton's Alchemical works, economist John Maynard Keynes observed that "Newton was not the first of the age of reason, he was the last of the magicians."[6] Don't count us out, John, there are still a few of us left.

Colin Wilson, as far as I'm concerned, wrote the definitive book on magic. If you had to ask him to define *magic*, he would tell you it's "the ability to live life guided by intuition." Ultimately, the most essential faculty you have to apply in using your *Intuition* as a coherent, practical mode of awareness is your imagination. And here's why: When you go into *In No Sense* and you *Observe the Obvious*, *Genius* information is going to occur to you, but not in plain English (or whatever your native tongue is) or in regular thoughts and feelings. *Perception*, your *Egoic* mode of awareness, has that advantage. It's a solid, trustworthy, familiar companion you understand plainly. Being immersed in your *Perception* is as natural to you as it is for fish to live in water. It is communicated in a language you speak every day and emotions whose meaning you've had internalized for ages, and, very conveniently, it has its roots in a long chain of evidentiary experience.

Intuition isn't that elegant, at all. It comes out of the dark nether regions of your psyche, where it lives in semi or permanent exile. It's like a child who grew up with the wolves, who comes out of the forest one day naked and wild-eyed, without any practice in the language of her human society. She has no words to describe a reality others can't relate to anyway. *Intuition* is *not* a neat and full package of

---

[6] John Maynard Keynes, "Newton, the Man", The Royal Society Newton Tercentenary Celebrations 15–19 July, 1946 (Cambridge: Cambridge University Press, 1947), p. 27.

comprehensible information contained in structured words and logic. It has to rely on symbolism, a kind of sign language comprising what I referred to earlier: the gut feeling, the curious sense of something, vague impressions, snippets of obvious knowing, symbolic association, imagery, colors or lights, physical sensations, energetic frequencies. Yet, just because it might be crude and vague on first impression, do not underestimate *Intuitive* symbolism—it is packed with tons of detail. It just has to be unpacked—translated—interpreted. Which is where the imagination comes in. We coax out the tangible, practical information imbedded in whatever symbols we are apprehending by *making up what they mean*.

That is why I'm surprised Casanova was so freaked out when the prophesies he made up came true. Anyone who studies and practices Alchemy should appreciate the power of the imagination, and from there it shouldn't be too big a leap to click that the most obvious way in which we use our imagination is *making things up*. If we are looking for insight into anything, we only have to make it up. As we get our imagination going, it's as if we begin pedaling a psychic contraption that sweeps up in the ethers all the known truth available concerning whatever we have put our attention on, and then funnels it into our *Self Conscious* awareness. The more bold and specific we can be, the more accurate and profound will the information we formulate turn out to be.

What we start getting will often seem outrageous to us—so irrational—in that it might not be what we want to know, or it can apparently contradict what we are currently sure of, or just that we can't see how it could be true. But if you want to build your *Super Conscious* muscles, you have to stop trying to make sense and start going with what you get. Don't forget, what unwittingly made Casanova such a great psychic was his proclivity for being as outrageous as he could be. After all, does this not remind us of my friend Theo, who embarrassed me by making up the most outrageous accusations about our potential sponsor's character, which the property developer himself ended up acknowledging were true?

I know of many wealth and business experts and

Personal and Spiritual Development gurus who allude to the power of the imagination and the importance of applying it to achieve inspired end results and more exalted states of mind and being, yet I don't know of anything that any of them do specifically to help people actually engage their imaginations in any meaningful way. In the work I teach, re-engaging the imagination and developing a natural working relationship with it is a top priority. One of the processes I use is the *Symbol Interpretation Exercise*. It may sound simple (and it is) but it takes a lot of guts to dive into. As a developmental practice, we start off with people working in pairs formulating information about their partners, whom they usually haven't met before. The participant makes an intention regarding what they want to know about their partner—their health, say, or their vocational life, maybe—and then makes an intention for some image or even just a sense of something to come to them. Something will then come to them, and from there their job is to go wild making up what the symbol means to them. Everyone is always blown away by how accurate their delivery is, especially in light of how wrong it feels to say, especially at the start.

Back in the day when I started running *Intuition* workshops, I used to make a deal with my participants whereby I offered them their money back for the weekend if they went all-out interpreting their symbol, and by the end their partner honestly could say that the reflection they got of themselves was less than seventy-five percent accurate. I never once had to give anyone their money back. Everyone has a *Genius*. Though, to achieve that level of accuracy in an intuitive reading, there are some conventions that have to be adhered to. These are some of the main ones to remember:

1. Always choose to be of service to whomever or whatever you are looking at. That is just a good value to begin with, and it takes the attention off of you and how you think you have to "perform."

2. Make an intention about the end result of the reading. Give your *Subconscious* a clear instruction of your objective.

3. Go into *In No Sense*. Let go of what you think you know, and let go of needing to know or be right. Be in the mystery. Be in awe.

4. Choose for a symbol to come to you that relates to your intention.

5. Go with whatever symbol you get. Don't question it or look for a better one. Intuition is the *first* thing you get, and when you go past that, you corrupt the whole process.

6. Never assume you don't have a symbol. Everything is a symbol. Every picture, every sense of something, any snatch of direct knowing, a flash of color, whatever is going on in your mind, even if it's blank, that's a symbol.

7. Notice what is obvious about the symbol. Make up what it means based on what is obvious to you. Don't rely on universal symbolism you learned from Jung or anyone else. Let that go. It's what it obviously means to you personally.

8. Make it up.

9. Don't wait for the meaning to come to you. It will come only once you begin talking.

10. Start talking. Keep talking. Don't stop talking. There is something about talking that activates the imagination. Edgar Cayce, the famous medical intuitive and arguably the most renowned psychic in history, claimed that our voice is the highest vibration in the human consciousness. As you talk and start to feel the flow of wisdom come on, you'll understand why he said that.

11. Don't describe the symbol. Just deliver the meaning.

12. Don't judge what you are getting. Don't compare.

13. Don't need or wait for it to make sense.

14. Be specific. Instead of saying "someone," make up who exactly. Instead of saying "something," make up exactly what. Fluffy, general information doesn't help you nail the truth and formulate meaningful information. When you try this out for yourself, you'll see that it does take guts to really lean into and make up stuff regardless of whatever reservations are coming up for you. There is not much we fear more than being wrong. And to be wrong through our own fault is even worse. *Egoically*, that means our orientation is unreliable—and don't forget, as far as our *Ego* is concerned, orientation is the most essential aspect of survival.

I did mention right at the outset that we are subject to some appalling assumptions that retard our creative expression and thereby our potential to live an empowered and joyful life. I've already pointed out a few doozies, and here's another one: making things up is bad. Which child hasn't been put down with, "You're just making that up"? In our culture that is a terrible slight. Think about it for a moment. It doesn't just mean that your contribution has no validity, it suggests that it is on a par with lies and falsehoods. It's bad. You're bad. What becomes important, then, is being in possession of and communicating only safe, unassailable information, which generally means what everyone else will believe and agree with. *Unconsciously*, you end up relating to your own wisdom, the truth you realize for yourself, as embarrassing nonsense. And when you're stuttering in your first attempts to tap into your *Genius* by making up what a symbol means, see if you can tell me I'm wrong.

In our society we are poisoned against the most beautiful part of ourselves, the diamond of our beings. We see our imaginations as an unreliable vestige of our primordial selves that should have dropped off with our monkey tails. Many would argue my point, saying no, they value imagination. Yes, mostly as it relates to flamboyant style, maybe, or in an artistic sense, or as a storytelling capacity, but not as the bedrock of our personal greatness. Not as the sacred vessel of our sovereign truth. That is something we all have to learn to reclaim and make a stand for if we intend to raise our creative capacity. I can't think of a bigger impediment to operating from *Genius* than the inherited shame we feel in connection with our personal wisdom. At some point we have to grow up and give ourselves permission to know and express our authentic, self-generated truth. Or else we risk staying stuck in our *Conforming Tendencies* and *Egoic Perceptions*, stuck at the level of *Imitation* or *Derivative* —forever.

    I'm very familiar with psychic cringe. I've seen it in thousands of clients and I recognize it in myself. It's a great leveler. People who are apparently very accomplished in their given fields, or outwardly seem to have it together, all have a meltdown when confronted with relying exclusively on their innate knowing for the first time. Learning to trust your own *Genius* is a function of practice. If you're dedicated to creating on a *High-Level Creative Frequency*, you'll soon figure out what works and what doesn't. I know for myself, my *Intuition* has guided me along a very blessed path in life, and it's the painful mistakes that I have made that keep me on the razor's edge of a diligent *Super Conscious* practice. Hopefully by sharing with you the benefit of my experience with *Creativity* and *Intuition*, you can avoid many of the pitfalls I encountered on my journey. So, let me conclude this chapter on *Intuition* with a cautionary tale.

    A friend of mine—let's call him Michael—is a wealthy wheeler-dealer who unbeknownst to me had a grudge against another close friend of his who happened to be a self-made billionaire. The billionaire—we'll call him Ross— had more money than Michael, more property than Michael, more cars than Michael, was a better surfer than Michael, knew more about wine than Michael, was a more accomplished horseman than Michael, beat him at tennis, could fly airplanes, had a beauty queen for a wife, and in fact there was nothing Michael could rival Ross at. But that wasn't Michael's problem with him. It was the billionaire's arrogance, the fact that he never let a chance go to establish his superiority and everyone else's inferiority. So Michael wanted to do something to cut Ross down a peg, and he figured he would use me for that purpose. Even though it was still fairly early in my career as a Creative Development trainer, I already had something of a formidable reputation as an intuitive counselor. Michael knew that when I counseled anyone, part of the picture I gave them was what they were playing out dysfunctionally. He figured that if he organized for me to do a session with Ross, I'd give him a good serving about what was wrong with him.

I didn't know any of this. I would never knowingly allow my expertise to be used in attacking someone else's character. All I knew was that Michael had organized for me to do a reading on this guy Ross, whom I knew only by reputation. I have to admit, though, I did see working with such a prominent figure as an opportunity to enhance my own fame. Consequently, I was in good spirits as Michael drove me to the appointment at Ross's mansion. But once we entered through the electronic gates and motored down the drive lined with luxury cars and past stables full of Arabian stud horses, I could feel the butterflies starting to flap around in my stomach. My psychic cringe was coming on. I hadn't even met my client, but judging by his domain, I was starting to doubt that I might have anything worthwhile to offer someone of his stature.

Michael dropped me off outside the front door of the mansion and drove away, promising to fetch me in a couple of hours. I innocently assumed his parting call of "Go get him," were words of encouragement rather than a vindictive directive. A handsome man attired in smart, casual clothes opened the door and introduced himself as the butler. He led me down a wide travertine-tiled corridor, past sumptuous living spaces, game rooms, and home entertainment theatres. I recognized a few Picassos on the walls, and I didn't get the feeling they were anything other than originals. After a seemingly endless walk, we arrived at a massive open-plan kitchen-dining area where Ross's trophy wife was pouring *Moët* for a coterie of bikini-clad beauties, the shortest one of whom would have been six inches taller than me. The lady of the house greeted me with a disarming smile. "Hi! You must be the psychic." It wasn't a genuine welcome. She didn't seem to know what our relationship should be, so she resolved the awkward silence that followed by holding out a bubbling flute. "Would you like some champagne?"

Maybe I should explain that my mother comes from Hungarian aristocracy. She's a very egalitarian woman who dedicated most of her life to tirelessly improving the welfare of those less fortunate than herself. But she sometimes does betray a hint of snobbery, especially when she refers to the more Bohemian types in society as "circus people." If you hear her use the term, you know it's no compliment. And if I think of all the misfits in the circus—the geeks and the clowns and the bearded lady—I imagine that, in my mother's eyes, the psychic would be pretty much at the bottom of the heap. In my own mind, being announced as "the psychic" downgraded my standing even more. I declined the glass of champagne, not just because it was only ten in the morning—I also felt I had better keep my intuitive wits about me.

With a crystal tumbler of water in hand, I was led to a sumptuously furnished glassed-in patio situated at the shallow end of an indoor-outdoor swimming pool. From where I sat, I had a one-hundred-and-eighty-degree view of the ocean. The tranquil vista beyond the manicured gardens did nothing to calm my performance anxiety. My heart was racing, my palms were sweaty and I had a lump in my throat. Meeting the billionaire himself was even more daunting an experience than I had anticipated. He swept peremptorily into the sunroom, talking loudly on his phone, letting the person on the other end know that he was attending to a trivial matter and would be available again shortly. He was a heavyset man, to say the least, with a chunk of crudely carved granite for a head. The centerpiece of his opulent look was a flowing snow-white Versace shirt emblazoned with bunches of purple grapes and gold chains. A pair of mirrored sunglasses was fixed to his gargoyle face, batting back all reflection to where it came from. He wore a big, gold

Rolex watch, with diamond-encrusted bracelets and rings. Lowering his ample frame into a chair opposite me, he set up a tape recorder on the glass table between us. He sat back grandiosely and spread his arms wide to invite my best shot. "So, what can you tell me?" he smirked. "It's obvious that I'm rich, isn't it?" I swallowed. This gauche brute, ensconced in his modern-day palace, seemingly complete with a harem, was the most formidable person I had ever met in my life. I felt compelled to dig deep and come up with something really impressive.

My own sense of inadequacy wasn't by itself my undoing—it had some help. It's not unusual, even to this day, that I feel confronted when I'm tuning into someone, regardless of who they are. I don't give it the power. I always let *In No Sense* take care of whatever's disturbing me. With Ross, I did what I always do: I acknowledged my discomfort, chose to serve him, let go of my assumptions about him, and asked for a symbol to come to me. A picture of a guitar immediately came to mind—and that was what did me in.

In the days leading up to my session with Ross, I had been working with a band, preparing the musicians creatively to record their latest album. My first thought was that the sessions I had done with them were muddling what I wanted to see about Ross. Which led to my second and most damning thought, that even if the symbol did relate to the tycoon, talking music with a man so focused on material and commercial matters would not offer him any useful insight. I made the fatal mistake that I tell everyone I teach not to make: I dismissed the symbol I was given and asked for another one that would make more sense and fit my agenda. From then on images did come, but talking about them led nowhere. I gave a painfully stilted reading. If I'm honest, I drew more on the signs I saw around me than on my own *Super Conscious* knowing. I was manipulating Ross with flattery, rather than giving him an honest insight.

The reading lasted twenty minutes instead of the full hour we had booked. In fact, we didn't even conclude formally. During an uncomfortable lull in my delivery the big man began playing with the On-Off button on his phone, and when it rang, he walked outside to answer it and never came back. After a painfully long wait, the butler appeared to see if I needed anything. Sensing my distress, he asked if I wanted to be shown out. I followed him through the mansion again feeling like a returning warrior of a defeated army who wished he had died in battle. When Michael finally arrived to pick me up, he was incredulous that I had not managed to find any flaws in Ross's armor. As if I didn't feel bad enough, I had to listen to him for half an hour furiously rattling off all the things I should have found fault with in his so-called best friend.

That wasn't the end of it, either. Knowing exactly what Michael had been playing at, shortly after my session Ross invited a group of psychology and psychiatry professors from neighboring universities to his house and played them back the tape of my reading. They all concurred that it was gibberish, and even provided written reports judging what they had heard to be completely void of any professional or clinical substance whatsoever. Ross then passed the reports on to Michael. Not only that, he also circulated them among their circle of friends, some of whom were acquainted with me. I ran into one of the recipients at the post office one day and she was highly amused by the incident. "I hear you broke your teeth on Ross," she laughed. My humiliation was absolute.

I was so anguished at having failed Michael and being the laughing stock of the Who's Who in town that I called on a peer of mine hoping he could give me a higher perspective of the debacle. I had hardly finished telling him the story before he cut in. "That Ross is a total asshole," he sneered. "I knew him long before he went into business. He's got a real chip on his shoulder. He had a dream of becoming a rock star and he failed. He sucked big time. Now he pays rock stars to hang out with him." What I was hearing made me sick. I wanted to get up and smash my head against the wall. The image of that guitar came back to me. I remembered it clearly—a blue Dobro similar to the one on the cover of Dire

Straits' *Brothers in Arms*. Two things were clear to me: firstly, if I had followed through on that symbol I would have ended up giving Ross a profound insight into himself and his powerlessness around his own passion; and secondly, he wouldn't have wanted a panel of shrinks to hear what I had to say—it would have cut too close to the bone. It might even have given Michael satisfaction, not that that truly mattered to me. Nowadays if I'm tempted to second-guess an intuitive impression, I only have to recall that disastrous experience to man up and play the hand I've been dealt.

GUIDANCE

Although I did say that my cautionary tale would be my last word in concluding this chapter, I would be remiss in not passing on a vital—and practical—tool for developing your *Intuition*. Just about the most effective exercise I give my students to practice their *Intuition* with is *Spirit Guidance*. It's a very powerful premise that incorporates all three disciplines of *Intuition*: *In No Sense*, *Observing the Obvious*, and *Making It Up*. The only significant distinction is that it substitutes writing for speaking, which makes it a much less confronting exercise. It's based on a shamanic technique that is designed to get you out of your left-brain and put you in a state of *Super Conscious* receptivity. I'll also give you a link to my *Spirit Guidance Visualization*, but first I just want to describe the process and explain how it works.

You need to find some quiet time and a quiet, comfortable place conducive to a meditative state. You also have to have a pen and paper standing by (typing into an electronic device also works, but actual hand-writing seems to work better, having almost the same intuitive effect as speaking does). A good practice to start with is grounding yourself by being mindful of what's going on for you—in your life, in your body, and in your thoughts and feelings. There's nothing to resolve or fix, just notice. Then imagine you're walking through a forest. Really allow yourself to actively build a full-sensory experience. Imagine vividly, as best you can, every detail of the forest: the sights, the sounds, the scents, even the feel of the earth underfoot or things you brush up against. Then imagine you find a path leading through the forest, and you begin following it. You keep noticing and building a sense of what it's like walking through the forest. You arrive at a fork in the path and you take the left fork. You keep picturing yourself walking along this path in the forest. It leads to a clearing of violet flowers. You walk out into the clearing, and imagine you've walked so far into it that when you look around there's nothing but a sea of violet all around you. Even the forest has disappeared. You walk for a little while through the field of violet flowers until you notice an edifice on the horizon. You begin walking towards it. As you get closer you realize that it's some kind of temple or equally hallowed place. Soon it looms before you and you go inside. It's important that you climb a set of stairs and enter through a definite portal, such as a doorway or a gateway or an arch. Finally, you find your way to a hall or atrium at the center of this sacred building, where you will meet your *Spirit Guide*.

I'll deal with the conventions of *Spirit Guidance* shortly, but let me cover the most important one now. You're making all of this up. Are there such things as *Spirit Guides*? Maybe, maybe not. If you believe in them, fine. If not, also fine. At the very least, they are a premise for contact with your own *Super Conscious* wisdom. By acting as if they are real and the process is valid, you are going to create the powerful result of developing your *Intuition* as well as gaining insights and foresight you otherwise likely would never come by. So, if you start thinking, "This is crazy," get over it and have some fun making it up.

Now it's time to meet your *Guide*. You imagine some entity emerging from the wings of the space you're in. You greet each other, and you ask your *Guide* to tell you what they can about whatever it is you want guidance on. The *Guide* then touches your head, which transforms into a sphere of light, and they begin telling you everything they know. At this time, you pick up your pen and paper (or your electronic device) and begin writing down what you imagine them to be telling you. And you keep writing until you feel complete.

That's the process. All the rules of *Intuition* and *Symbol Interpretation* apply. Here are some further tips that apply specifically to, or more especially to, *Spirit Guidance*:

1. When you meet a *Guide*, they can take any form, from an amoeba to Archangel Gabriel to a hedgehog. What form they take doesn't matter—as long as they can talk. You have to imagine them talking. And, by the way, more than one can appear, though do focus on establishing who the lead *Guide* is and getting guidance mainly from them.

2. Make it up!

3. As with any *Intuition* technique, don't question what you're getting. Don't worry whether the information is credible or not, sensible or not, new or not—just write it down. Don't stop writing until you're complete.

4. It is totally appropriate that you ask your *Guides* questions of general interest; however, you'll have a tendency to want your guides to resolve your dilemmas, and your relationship with *Guidance* can become bound in your *Egoic* agendas. Once that happens you will begin channeling garbage. To avoid this, make sure that in every *Guidance* session you have at least one general, open-ended question, like: "What guidance will serve my highest good?" or "How can I be true to myself?" This creates the space for true *Intuition*, which is information that has flowed undirected by any *Egoic* preoccupation.

5. Make a religious habit of reading guidance two weeks after you have written it. At first your guidance might not have the ring of truth—quite the opposite maybe—but as you begin checking it in retrospect, you will be amazed at the integrity of your *Guides*.

No other process will develop your *Intuition* as powerfully as *Spirit Guidance*. If you do it regularly enough—I recommend twice a week—your *Intuition* will become more and more integrated as a normal mode of awareness, rather than something you check in with reactively. In my book *The Magician's Way*, I wrote that you can't stick a straw into the magician's world and hope to suck energy out of it—you have to stand in the magician's world if you mean to live by magic. Well, if you want to live on your *Highest Creative Frequency*, you can't expect to retain your *Low-Level Creative Frequency* awareness and then perform pseudo mystic-scientific rituals in the hope of causing *Genius* creations. That's the definition of superstition. Positive thinking, positive affirmations, an attitude of gratitude, and all ideas about how you can safely get something for nothing—other than merely adopting a spiritually or morally correct way of being—won't empower you in any meaningful way. In fact, they are more likely to have the opposite effect. You need to learn how to plug into your *Super Conscious* mode of awareness and live your life guided by that. Ultimately, developing your *Intuition* to a masterful level doesn't take anywhere near as much energy as learning a foreign language. But even if it did, wouldn't you make that investment if it meant living your life as an expression of your highest potential? (For an audio of the Spirit Guide Meditation, please go to williamwhitecloud.com/naturalsuccessbonus/).

CHAPTER FOUR
THE FOURTH STEP OF NATURAL SUCCESS

FOLLOWING THROUGH

I am not a hero worshipper by any means, but whenever I am asked to name the historical figure I most admire, I have no hesitation in nominating Harriet Tubman. I can't think of anyone whose reputation I admire more. Tubman was born a slave in Dorchester County, Maryland, in 1822. If you've seen the Oscar-winning movie *12 Years a Slave*, you will appreciate the brutal reality of slavery. Tubman endured the same vile treatment meted out to her counterparts in that film. As a child she was beaten and whipped by a succession of masters. When she was only a little girl, she suffered a traumatic head wound caused by an irate slave owner who threw a heavy metal weight intending to hit another slave but which cracked her skull instead. The blow caused dizziness, pain, and spells of hypersomnia, which she suffered throughout her entire life. An additional side effect of the injury, apparently, was the strange visions and vivid dreams she experienced from then on.

Tubman escaped to Philadelphia in 1849, and then immediately returned to Maryland to rescue her family. Nor did she stop at saving her relatives. Once she had brought her family to safety, she continued guiding dozens of other slaves to freedom. Travelling at night in extreme secrecy, Tubman undertook thirteen treacherous missions to rescue seventy enslaved family members and friends. Using a network of antislavery activists and safe houses known as the Underground Railroad, she brought them by foot from the South all the way to Canada, then known as British North America. During the Civil War, Tubman served the Union Army, first as a cook and nurse and then as a scout and spy. She was the first woman to lead an armed expedition in the war. In one of her most noted exploits, she guided the Raid at Combahee Ferry in South Carolina, which liberated more than seven hundred slaves. On April 20, 2016, the U.S. Department of the Treasury announced its intention to replace Andrew Jackson's portrait with that of Tubman's on America's twenty-dollar bill.

Looking at a photo of "Moses" (Harriet Tubman's nickname), I see the faces of the African trackers I grew up with in hers. There's the fierce countenance mitigated by soulful eyes, which draw you into a compassionate embrace with all of existence. That look tells you everything about her character. To me, it is not so remarkable that she was guided by her dreams every step of the way, or that she never lost one of her charges in any of her perilous escapes, all of which were practically suicide missions. I already know that our *Natural Ability* can serve us in achieving the most incredible end results. We all have it in us. No, to me, what is so remarkable is that she followed her *Super Conscious* guidance so faithfully. Because the one thing I know about human nature is that the will to follow through on our truth is generally our weakest attribute, a serious drawback considering it is also the most important determinant in being able to live on a *High-Level Creative Frequency*. As they say in the East, "To know and not do is to still not know."

When *The Magician's Way* first took off, it was entirely thanks to one man, the Sydney wealth-creation guru Roy McDonald. He was browsing in a bookstore in my then hometown of Byron Bay two days after it had been released. My book literally fell off a shelf right in front of him. Roy picked it up and looked it over, intrigued by the title. On the strength of the endorsement by a mutual friend on the cover, he bought the same copy he had picked up off the floor. He read the story cover to cover in one sitting, and was so impressed with it that he called his personal assistant and instructed her to buy a hundred copies and send them out as gifts to the top members of his network. The recipients of his gift were mostly leaders of significant networks themselves, and many of them in turn recommended the book to their memberships. The rest is history. When I finally met Roy, I asked him why he had been so impressed by *The Magician's Way*. "The chapter on taking action," he told me. "I can teach people the principles of wealth creation, but I can't teach them to take the necessary action."

I'd like you to think back to the story of my friend Fergus Herbert, who parlayed two dollars into a business conglomerate whose core enterprise employed seventy people and turned over twenty million dollars a year. To some it might sound easy. Well, they'd think, he had an inspiring idea, he put it to his friends, then just waited calmly until the right opportunity came along. Think again. Think about every sense of inspiration Fergus had to receive—to pay attention to and act on—in spite of many doubts and fears, for that end result to materialize. First, he had to acknowledge the significance of three quality professionals calling him on the same day inquiring about work. He could have dismissed it as a sheer coincidence, a sign of the hard economic times. In fact, here he might have gone into reaction and begun to worry about the viability of his existing projects and developments. Instead, Fergus sat with the significance of the coincidence, and the sense that he and the other three shared a combined destiny. Right about now, he could have—and ninety-nine out of a hundred would have—talked himself out of that idea. He had enough on his plate, and why should he be responsible for the others? They were powerful creators; they'd land on their feet. On top of all of that, what could they do together? Fergus didn't want to start a business just for the sake of it, and have to pour money into something to resolve his friends' dilemmas.

Let me tell you, I happen to know Fergus well. Put an idea to him and he'll slice and dice it with a logic that will make your head spin. In the life of a busy wheeler-dealer, the fancy of getting some undefined enterprise going with three other random businessmen could easily have been dismissed in favor of a host of urgent matters calling for his attention. But it's the notion that occurred to Fergus next that was truly preposterous: they would create something from nothing. That was about as audacious as pitching *Seinfeld*—a television show about nothing. Why bother with the unknown when real deals were on the table? And what about the other three? How could Fergus in all seriousness expect men battling to pay their mortgages and provide for their families to risk giving up their quest for gainful employment and undertake an experiment in magic? What would they think of him for even suggesting the idea? Surely they would laugh in his face, reject his proposal out of hand. Who needed that kind of aggravation and responsibility? It didn't make sense. It was the rational equivalent of ignoring real birds in the hand and chasing after the possibility of an invisible bird in the bushes. The path of least resistance would be to just shrug off the hare-brained whim and get on with actual business at hand.

Just consider all the tension points and barriers arising from there. Picking up the phone and inviting each executive to meet. Putting the proposal to them. Standing strong in the face of their initial outrage and skepticism. Committing to pay their salaries for a year without a shred of certainty that anything would come of his scheme. Guaranteeing to provide the necessary capital. Hanging with everyone's tension as they manically tried to force unsuitable projects on each other. Dealing with their disappointments and negativity and, towards the end, their despair. All along wondering whether these men had what it took, whether he had made the right decision, whether he shouldn't do the right thing by them and himself and just call the whole thing off.

Fergus only had to stumble and lose heart at one of many steps for his end result to fade like a mirage in the desert sands. Even the call Fergus made to go and see Gill, the man who gave them the magazines that were to become the cornerstone of their success, was vital to the end result. Fergus didn't know why Gill wanted to see him. That the publisher might have something for the Knights of the Round Table was the furthest thing from his mind. He'd never had business dealings with Gill, nor had he ever assumed that he would. Fergus was under no obligation to take up the businessman's invitation, and if he did feel inclined he could have done so at some convenient time in the future—maybe had lunch with him when his calendar permitted. But Fergus had a feeling that there was something significant about the offer, and he acted on that instinct. He went and saw Gill first thing the next morning.

When we look at the accomplishments of others—the books they wrote, the businesses they created, the money they made, the awards they won, the practices they mastered, the change they affected, the love they found—we tend to overlook the energy that went into those accomplishments; we tend to think of them as something that just inevitably happened. We might give credit to the *Genius* involved, but rarely do we appreciate the *Will* it took. As the diva complained to the journalist, "People are saying I'm an overnight success, but I was working my butt off for ten years before I made it." That is why I don't disparage, scorn, or envy the good fortune of others. It is a profound achievement to recognize a possibility in life or within yourself and take ownership of that possibility, to the point that you see it through regardless of any inner or outer resistance that you may encounter.

NEGREDO, ALBEDO, RUBEDO

It may already be apparent to you that much of my *Natural Success* model has been informed by the principles of Alchemy. For most people, Alchemy is an arcane subject. In my experience, even those who appreciate it as an esoteric system for human transformation don't have a clear understanding of what it's really about and how it works. Though scholars often attempt to interpret the psychological significance of Calcination, Dissolution, Separation, Conjunction, Fermentation, Distillation, and Coagulation, the principles of Alchemy remain inaccessible to the average person, a kind of romantic reference, at best. But really, to appreciate Alchemy for the creatively transformative process that it is and to apply it practically, you only have to understand the significance of *Negredo*, *Albedo*, and *Rubedo* as the three phases of elemental transmutation, and also the meaning of the Hermetic axiom "You make the fixed volatile and the volatile fixed."

Negredo is a symbol for our *Unconscious* framework. It is represented by the color black, likely a metaphor for the "shadow" or Dark Side of human nature. Its astrological correspondent is Saturn, which represents fixed, masculine structure, most significantly our *Egoic* identity.

Albedo is a symbol for our *Super Conscious* nature. It is represented by the color white, here an obvious metaphor for our light side. Its astrological correspondent is Venus, representing the volatile, feminine, imaginative soul.

Rubedo is a symbol for our *Will*. It is represented by the color red. Its astrological correspondent is Mars, representing another side of the masculine, in this case passionate action and earthly tangibility.

The first stage of Alchemy (*Calcination*) and first phase (*Negredo*) finds us in our fixed, immutable manifestation, subject to our *Egoic Perception* and worldview. From there we make the fixed volatile; through the process of *Putrefaction* we break down that concrete, stuck state of mind. Going into *In No Sense* allows us to rise up into the light where we are informed by our inherent connection to everything through all time and space. In *Albedo* we transcend the boundaries of our preset two thousand-bit understanding and become receptive to *Super Conscious* realizations. But these insights and inspirations, as we well know, fade very quickly, subject as they are to the tyranny of rationalization.

The difference between a genius and everyone else, I've been told, is that the genius writes everything down. If we are to hold ourselves on our *High-Level Creative Frequency* we have to develop the ability to make the volatile fixed, which means cultivating the habit of transforming our fleeting dream-like knowing into tangible *Self Conscious* reality. In Alchemy they say that there is no gold until the red tincture—the fixing agent—is applied. But there's more to it than observing the obvious. Without completing the final phase of *Rubedo*—taking action—there is no manifestation of our truth. We have to remember, our dreams are not the gold; it is the dream manifested into reality that is the gold. Of all the phases of Alchemy, *Negredo* is the easiest to achieve—it's your default setting. *Albedo* takes some training, as you might appreciate after reading the previous chapter. But mastery of *Intuition* still does not make you a *Creative Master*. Mastering *Rubedo*—receiving and following through on inspiration—is what it ultimately takes.

OWNING YOUR TRUTH

I don't know if you can think back as far as the days before Facebook and Twitter, when email was the closest thing we had to social media? It seems so long ago now. Back then there was a type of nuisance email we used to get called a chain letter. For those of you who might not know, it was a kind of meme containing mythical or false information, which manipulated you through sympathy or fear to forward it on to your contact list. An example of the sympathy version would be an email saying that some poor child (abject picture attached) was dying of a rare illness and that a big corporation—Microsoft, say—was donating one dollar to the child's treatment for every person the letter was forwarded to. The scare version, whatever its message might be, would always end with examples of the good fortune that had come to people who had forwarded the letter, and horrible things that had happened to people who had refrained.

Please forgive me if I sound like I'm using that chain mail scare tactic here. But it's no manipulative tactic, just the truth. When you receive *Super Conscious* direction and you don't follow through on it, great misfortune is going to befall you. And by the same token, when you do follow through on *Genius* guidance, marvels beyond your wildest imagination will materialize. The biggest difference between a *Creative Master* and a dilettante is that the *Master* religiously follows through on their truth, by which I mean their *Super Conscious* awareness. It's a core value, part of the code they live by. They know full well the consequences of taking each step as it reveals itself...or not. For the dilettante, the truth is optional. They don't see the harm in keeping their mouth shut when their truth might be uncomfortable to express; they don't think it matters if they let a chance go by; or if they give up on something they want if it's a little hard, or think it's a luxury they don't have to have anyway, or fear others won't approve; or they don't act on their *Intuition* because it doesn't make sense or they can't see the benefit.

If you want to live your life on a *High-Level Creative Frequency* and enjoy a consistent flow of *Natural Success*, then you're going to need to adopt a new code to live by, which means you're going to value every crumb of truth your *Super Conscious* offers you. While the adage "To know and not do is to still not know" might be very true, it does not fully convey the life-defeating, soul-destroying repercussions of not acting on your truth, regardless of how consequential or inconsequential it appears to be. I know many individuals who constantly tune in to things and then never heed what their *Intuition* tells them. If that is going to be your relationship with your *Genius* then it's better you don't use your *Intuition* at all. I am serious! That is a game played by people whom the Alchemists used to refer to as the half-wise, who sooner or later are dashed against the rocks by reason of their own folly. And don't worry, before the end of this chapter, I'm going to make very clear why rigorous follow-through is so important and, in the final chapter, show you how taking right action can become an effortless practice, an ingrained behavior even.

Intuition is, in fact, a great analogy for creating. When you formulate information regarding something you want to know about, you first go into *In No Sense*, and from there you observe every detail of whatever becomes obvious, no matter how subtle or palpable it is. You can't have a discretionary relationship with whatever comes up; you can't take it or leave it. If you dismiss whatever you've been given and rather cast about for something more intelligible or impressive or in line with what you'd prefer to know, you corrupt the whole process. You go with what you get and unpack it without fear or favor. That's called owning and acting on your truth. We know that our *Intuition* is only as efficacious as our commitment. And so, the principles that apply to formulating intuitive information apply equally to living our lives guided by *Intuition*.

SHIT DOESN'T JUST HAPPEN

I consider myself lucky that very early on my path of exploring *Natural Success* I went on a journey that profoundly taught me to be unswerving in my dedication to following through, as painful as part of the lesson was. In the winter of 1994 I had just begun running *Intuition* workshops for my counseling clients who wanted to learn how to tap into the psychic ability I demonstrated in my sessions with them. I was invited to run a workshop in the charming seaside town of South West Rocks, about five hours north of Sydney. The weekend before the event, I was enjoying lunch in the gardens of a riverbank café a short drive inland from the Rocks. It was a pleasant outing except for one detail: At another table in the garden, a short distance from me and my friends, sat a family of four: an old man I assumed was the grandfather, a middle-aged couple—obviously the parents—and their teenage daughter, whom I guessed to be fifteen or sixteen. I was greatly irritated by the girl. Her hair was cut in a style trendy at the time—shaved up the back of her head and chopped severely on the sides just below her ears—which I didn't think flattered her. She came across as extremely precocious, apparently dominating the conversation, while the adults indulged her with a fawning attention. But what I found most irksome was the fact that she was chain-smoking, and how, from the flamboyant way she held and tapped the ash from her cigarette, it evidently gave her an overblown sense of importance.

I did my best to ignore the girl and her family, but it wasn't easy seeing as though I was seated facing them. At some point a fresh bout of laughter broke out at their table. My skin crawled as I watched her exhale a big cloud of smoke and sit back with a big, self-satisfied grin, now a glass of wine and a cigarette in the same hand. I mumbled my disapproval to my luncheon companions, and as they turned to see what the fuss was about, I heard a voice in my head, as loud and distinct as if someone beside me had spoken: "You and this girl are going to live together." I literally shuddered. The idea was appalling to me. I was thirty-eight at the time and she was merely a child to my mind—a little twit at that. But I couldn't shake those prophetic words; they left me disquieted for days after.

The first day of the workshop rolled around. My host realized that she didn't have enough milk for teas and coffee, so I volunteered to run down to the shops and get some. As I pulled out of the driveway, a car was driving up to the house. I pulled over to let the vehicle through. As it edged past me, the driver waved her thanks. It was the girl from the riverbank café. "Huh," I thought, "she drives!" I also wondered what she was doing there, and did my best to suppress an odd sense of excitement at the thought she might be there to attend the event.

Her name was Christian Horlin, and it turned out she was actually nineteen years old. She was about to leave for America on the first leg of an around-the-world adventure, as is the tradition for Australian school-leavers. She had seen a flyer for the workshop in a crystal shop in town, and decided that sharpening her intuition might serve her on her travels. I was surprised by the maturity she displayed and how naturally she took to the work, and I soon changed my mind about her being a twit. After two days of deeply personal and transformative work, I came to appreciate the gifted and spirited person that she was, although I didn't feel a shred of romantic sentiment mingling in with my newfound respect for the girl. I still didn't like her haircut.

On the night the workshop finished I had been invited to a friend's house for dinner, but leaving the workshop venue proved to be awkward. Everyone had said their goodbyes and driven off, except for Christian, who was still hanging around with no visible intention of taking off. I got the sense that she didn't want the magical spell of the workshop energy to be broken. The irony that I now felt sympathy for this same person I had despised at a distance the weekend before was not lost on me. I didn't have the heart to get rid of her, so I ended up inviting her to join me for dinner. And I must admit, I was happy when she readily accepted my invitation.

Our host was a Chinese medicine practitioner, and she had cooked up a very tasty Cantonese meal. We all ate heartily and the conversation flowed cheerfully, focusing mostly on a postmortem of the workshop and the lessons learned. As I enjoyed the good food and company, I was also a little apprehensive that Christian would show some sensitivity and leave before I had to ask her to. It had been an intense weekend and I, for one, needed some space and a good rest. As it happened, my tension was unfounded; not long after dessert was served she announced that she had better be going. There was the usual round of hugs and expressions of mutual admiration typical of post-workshop farewells, and then I walked her to her car. We said our goodbyes, her thanking me for all the great learnings and me wishing her well on her travels. Then we hugged each other warmly. The degree of affection between us must have justified a friendly kiss, because our lips did meet. But instead of the light brush I expected, the kiss lingered just a little and then…she bit my lower lip. I was shocked, not just by her provocative move, but also by the repressed passion that was unleashed by it. Six weeks later Christian flew back from England to move in with me.

In those intervening weeks I was also travelling. While I was in South Africa attending a family wedding, some of my relatives recounted to me their recent adventures in the deserts of South West Africa, an area I had always dreamed of visiting. Their descriptions and stories evoked for me the Africa of my childhood, in which pristine lands teemed with wild animals, and San bushmen still lived immune from the twentieth century. I made up my mind to go there, and as soon as Christian and I were reunited, we began planning an expedition for the following year. The logistics of travelling on our own to all the places we wanted to visit were problematic, but we happened to find a safari company that took group tours along the exact route we intended to explore. We didn't fancy the idea of sharing the four-thousand-mile trek with a random bunch of strangers, so we put it out to our network and ended up enlisting another thirty adventurous souls, including Christian's father, Alan, and her brother, Max—oh, and Petra, the filmmaker whose suicidal tendencies I had helped to overcome.

In 1995 my life was just coming together again after hitting rock-bottom with the ten-year malaise I described earlier in these pages. One of the casualties of my long-term illness was my bank account, and spending the last few years establishing myself in my new vocation as an intuitive counselor and, more lately, as a workshop facilitator hadn't done much to repair it. While I wasn't rolling in money, I had no reason to complain, either. I was doing well enough to rent a harborside townhouse and lease a nice little convertible and look after my girl, whom I was madly in love with. But the safari did pose a thorny problem: I was earning enough to live on, but I had no savings. We planned to be away for twelve weeks, which meant we needed twelve thousand dollars for our travels and enough extra to cover my rent and lease payments for that period. On top of that, we would be broke when we returned—assuming we were able to manifest the money to go—so I had to come up with a plan to straightaway be earning some serious cash to cover our bills when we got back.

The reason I was committed to going ahead with the safari, in spite of not knowing where I'd find the money to pay for it, was because my *Spirit Guides* had repeatedly assured me that the necessary funds would materialize. They didn't tell me where the money would come from, but they were adamant that it would manifest. In fact, they were very insistent that I go. I didn't feel like I had any other choice than to practice what I preached and follow their guidance.

There is one aspect of their guidance I did ignore, though. When I asked them how I could best plan to create a flow of money when I returned, I found myself writing, "Plan as if you are never coming back." I checked in with them several times to get clear on their meaning, but the cryptic message never changed. "Plan as if you are never coming back." I interpreted that statement to mean that I should remain in Africa, the thought of which I rejected out of hand. The bitter taste of my colonial upbringing in Swaziland and my experiences of apartheid in South Africa still soured my perception of life in the motherland. While I loved being out in the wilds, hanging out with my family was painful. I considered them to be representative of the society they lived in: obnoxiously unconscious. The thought of being a full-time member of a toxic society again made me thoroughly depressed. There was no scenario I could imagine that would make sense of my guidance. I opted to ignore my *Spirit Guides* in this case, and went ahead with working out a viable plan for hitting the road running on my return to Australia.

Hanging with the tension of waiting for the money to appear was a real test of nerves. We had made a group booking for both the safari and the return flights to South Africa, where our journey was to begin. The safari company and my travel agent required everyone to be paid up in advance, though as the organizer of the tour I was as a matter of course given an extended deadline. While all thirty members of our party were fully paid up, Christian and I, the tour leaders, still didn't know how we were going to come up with the twelve thousand dollars we needed. I had a lot to be anxious about.

My first concern was letting down the travel companies who fully trusted that I, being the tour principal, must of all people be good for the money. My whole life had been spent desperately trying to prove that I could live up to my responsibilities. Secondly, everyone who had signed up for the safari was coming on the basis of their close connection to me, and the reassurance that they'd have an old Africa hand like me along to look after them. I couldn't bear to think of their shock and disappointment (and disparagement, even) when they discovered that I hadn't been able to get it together—me, Mr. You Can Create Whatever You Love. Thirdly, there was also the thought of failing Christian and her family, who were eagerly anticipating sharing the once-in-a-lifetime adventure with each other. I was terrified of how it would look to Christian if I wasn't able to vindicate her faith in me and the magic I had enrolled her in. And, of course, because of where I was in my life at that time, it was a crucial test of whether I had the power to make my dreams prevail over my circumstances.

As the deadline for paying for our flights loomed, I began checking in with my *Guides* daily for some kind of understanding of our situation. In the end, I wasn't even looking for a sign of the money; I was just hoping for a dignified excuse to drop out. Then, three days before the due date, I received an email from my mother that almost gave me a heart attack. She informed me that a relative in Europe was giving away a portion of his estate for tax reasons, and that he planned on giving me, his third cousin, thirty thousand Swiss francs. Doing my best not to sound ungracious, I replied explaining my predicament and asking my mother if she could persuade our kinsman to wire me the money immediately. On the day of the deadline I received notification of the transfer. I called my travel agent and explained the situation. She had no problem waiting a few more days. When the money landed in my bank account, the thirty thousand francs converted to twelve thousand and five Australian dollars. The bank charged five dollars for the transfer and I was left with exactly twelve thousand dollars. We were going to Africa with the exact amount we needed.

That safari turned out to be a profoundly life-changing, life-affirming experience for everyone who came along, and important for me in many ways. Christian and I went over to South Africa a little before the start of the expedition and I was able to spend some time with my father before he died of Parkinson's. He had shriveled into a frail and trembling version of his former self. His cantankerous demeanor had melted into a little-boy face beaming with vulnerability and love. It took a Herculean effort for him to get just a couple of words out, so mostly we sat with each other in silent appreciation. On the last day we were together, he beckoned feebly with one shaky finger for me to come over to him. He willed me with his tear-filled eyes to come up really close. It took him maybe five minutes to wheeze out just one sentence: "I'm glad you've found something to do with your life, Billy." Those were the last words my father ever spoke to me.

After visiting my parents, we rendezvoused with our band of merry adventurers in Cape Town, a spectacular city blessed with so many scenic wonders and cultural delights. On a blustery morning, we all piled into specially converted World War II army trucks and drove out of town hooting and cheering. We cruised up the Western Cape into the Namaqualand Desert, where the famed Namaqualand Daisies were in full bloom. From the edge of the road to the horizon, across valley floors and up hillsides—for hundreds of miles—the earth was carpeted with impressionistic swathes of red and orange and yellow and lilac. It was a breathtaking start to our journey. We crossed the Orange River into Namibia and made a beeline for the Namib Desert. I caught my first sight of wild gemsbok, the most glorious member of the Oryx family, as big as cattle with long, rapier horns and stunning black-and-white mask-like faces. Owing to the dry conditions we didn't see much game, but we were gobsmacked enough by imposing red and orange canyons and arroyos and mesas. Everything was oversized, as if we were traversing a landscape in the Land of Giants.

In the Namib Desert there wasn't a blade of grass, just earth-orange sand dunes—massive suckers, the biggest in the world. We camped at the foot of a mountainous dune. In the morning we climbed five miles to its summit, from where we could see for sixty miles in every direction. It was like looking down on an endless ochre mountain range. Come mid-morning it rained, the first precipitation recorded in that place in ten years. It was only a short, sharp shower, but enough to unlock the most luxurious earth-scented fragrance imaginable.

Our route took us past the Fish River Canyon, the second biggest canyon in the world after the Grand Canyon, through Windhoek, the capital of Namibia, and on to the Etosha Pan game park. We drove through endless wilderness, literally thousands of miles of uninhabited country. We slept in tents under a blaze of stars; the Milky Way was so vivid it looked like someone really had spilled a pail of milk across the sky. In the northern half of the country the land is less arid, the vegetation still quite sparse but very nutrient rich, supporting hoards of animals. Within a few short days we'd seen so many elephants and giraffes and baboons and ostriches and impalas and springboks that we weren't stopping to look at anything other than lions and cheetahs. Sometimes we'd camp beside waterholes, and in the evenings elephants and rhinos would come for a drink and a wallow. Every night we heard lions roaring and hyenas whooping. If anyone left anything made of leather outside their tent—shoes or a belt—the hyenas and jackals ate those articles, laces and buckles and all.

Our last night in Namibia found us camped along the Kavango River on the border with Angola. It was one of our most eventful stops. While I was downriver tiger fishing, a large contingent of our group was persuaded by some locals they met—who turned out to be diamond smugglers—that it was safe to swim across to the Angolan side of the river. They were lucky to not get taken by crocodiles, or get shot by the Angolan army patrol that turned them back from the opposite bank with AK-47s. Not many years before, fierce wars had raged in the same area.

The Kavango River drains a massive basin, including big chunks of Angola and Zambia, and then, instead of flowing to the sea, it heads inland into the Kalahari Desert in Botswana, where it culminates in a fifteen-thousand-square-mile swamp known as the Okavango Delta. It's riparian forested islands are home to masses of wildlife—especially elephant, buffalo, crocodile, and hippo—as well as Bantu tribespeople and Bushmen who pole themselves gondolier-style through the waterways in dugout canoes called mokoros.

Everyone agreed that the highlight of the trip was going into the Okavango Delta. We got there by cutting through the Caprivi Strip, a kind of no man's land between Angola, Zambia, Zimbabwe, Botswana, and Namibia, and then dropping down to Maun, a ramshackle town that serves as a gateway into the Okavango. Its most distinctive feature is a massive barrier surrounding the town to protect it from the annual buffalo migration. From Maun we were taken in four-wheel-drive vehicles to the edge of the swamps, and then ferried in shallow draught motorboats to an island encampment, beyond which motorized vehicles of any kind are not permitted. At the village we were split into three groups and then poled deep into the swamps in our mokoros by our native guides on a mind-blowing three-day Delta immersion.

I can't even begin to describe the beauty of the waterways, or the sensory overload of colorful birdlife, or the thrill of gliding silently by hippos and elephants low in the water. We had to keep big fires going in the dark to deter brazen lions and hyenas. That proved a problem in one of the camps when a rhino kept charging through the tents trying to stomp the fire out. (Sadly, rhinos, those firemen of the bush, are now extinct in the Delta due to poaching.) The only thing keeping us alive out there was the jungle smarts of our unarmed guides. On one of the nights, sitting around the fire, in front of the other campers, I asked Alan for his daughter's hand in marriage. I wasn't sure whether he was crying tears of joy or not, but he did give his blessing. When our guides heard that Christian and I had just become engaged, they pulled out lyre-like instruments and began singing us Tswana love songs. I don't think there was a dry eye in the camp.

The last leg of our journey took us through another renowned African game reserve—the Chobe Elephant Park—to the Victoria Falls in Zimbabwe. By way of a completion ceremony we did a sunset cruise on the Zambezi River, watching more hippos and elephants frolicking in water, and reminiscing about our fabulous adventures, with Amarula liqueurs in hand. One of the stories we had a good laugh about happened earlier that same day. A particular woman in our party had managed to create being attacked wherever we went on our trip (not the funny part, but talk about patterns of experience!), and while a bunch of us were standing in the queue at the little border post accessing the walking bridge between Zimbabwe and Zambia—which afforded a magnificent view of the thundering falls—this woman ran screaming hysterically past us and on to the bridge, in total disregard of the armed border guards. Before the startled guards had a chance to do anything, they were overrun by a whole troop of irate baboons in hot pursuit of the woman. Turns out she had been antagonizing the apes, thinking she was safe on the other side of a high wire-mesh fence. She hadn't seen the gaping hole in the mesh right beside her, which the baboons soon figured out was there.

Less amusing was the experience of travelling with Air Zimbabwe. When we were flying out of the Falls to take our respective paths home, there was a long delay before takeoff. Finally the captain came through the cabin with his cap out asking passengers to chip in for jet fuel; the airline's credit limit with the local fuel supplier was evidently overextended. If we'd had any sense we would have gotten off the plane there and then, but after weeks of living on the edge it didn't seem like a big deal.

Before we flew out, Christian went to see the local sangoma. He told fortunes in the traditional way by Throwing the Bones. His psychic powers were impressive, especially in retrospect. He told Christian that her family consisted of herself, a brother and a father and mother. He could see that her parents' marriage was in trouble. She was betrothed to a man older than herself, and she would have two children by him, a boy and a girl. The man has problems with his health. We couldn't say at the time about the boy and girl, but everything else was spot-on. How perceptive was he to know that I'd had health issues?

But that witch doctor wasn't talking about the past. When Christian and I got back to Australia a few months later, I got sick the day after we landed. The main symptom was a chest pain that intensified when I lay back and felt better when I sat up. Based on my overall condition, it felt to me that my hiatal hernia was playing up, presumably agitated by all the rich food we were eating in Africa. I bought some antacid medication and looked forward to the hernia calming down within a few days, which it normally did once I got a few bottles of Gaviscon® down my throat.

It didn't get better; it got worse. Being sick wasn't part of the plan—I was supposed to be doing counseling sessions and organizing workshops to replenish my depleted cash reserves. Hoping to speed my recovery, I went to see a doctor who agreed with my self-diagnosis, but he didn't think there was any more to be done than what I was already doing: resting and taking antacid tonics. Christian and I saw no point in hanging around in the city while I was incapacitated so we decided to go and stay with her parents in the country for a while. The drive nearly killed me. By the time we got to their place I hardly had the strength to walk from my car to the house. I lay in bed for a week in excruciating pain.

That I had a hiatal hernia seemed to be confirmed by the fact that the pain got worse after meals. Christian's mother,

Finola, was pushing for me to go to hospital, but I was resisting the idea because I was invested in going back to Sydney and sorting myself out—bills were mounting and clients were going unserviced. In the end, though, it reached the point where I couldn't eat a crumb without being attacked by violent chest pains and nausea. I was admitted to hospital, where the attending doctor also agreed with my self-diagnosis, and concurred that I only needed time to heal. He wasn't at all perturbed that I didn't improve in the ten days under his care and that I hadn't touched my food since being admitted.

So concerned was Christian by my deteriorating condition that she called a doctor friend of ours in Sydney, who organized for me to be discharged into the care of a colleague in the nearby city of Coffs Harbour. When I arrived at the doctor's rooms, I was doubled over in agony and trembling like a leaf. More than the pain, I was shaken to my core by the fear that some malevolent force I had no control over was once again dragging me into the abyss. The doctor took one look at me and said to his assistant, "This man has pericarditis." I was immediately taken for x-rays, which confirmed his diagnosis. Pericarditis is an inflammation of the heart lining, easily treated with cortisone, but usually fatal if not treated. In my case, I had already been ill for forty days before my condition had been diagnosed and any life-saving super steroids prescribed. It was touch-and-go whether I would live or die, and in the year it took me to convalescence I had plenty of time to appreciate the meaning of my guidance, "Plan as if you are never coming back."

As I said at the start of this story, that rollercoaster of an experience taught me everything I needed to learn about follow-through, and much about creating, for that matter. The biggest lesson for me was that our experiences in life are structural, not random or personal. Personal power and creative success are strictly born of an uncompromised connection to our *Super Conscious*, and struggle and suffering are a result of trying to resolve our *Egoic* identity. In the one instance, I had identified an end result I loved and remained faithful to my heart all the way through to completion, regardless of any inner or outer resistance. In the second instance, my sense of powerlessness had been triggered and I had failed to listen to what my *Unconscious* was telling me, thereby failing to neutralize that *Low-Level Creative* message and keep my *Super Conscious* channels open.

The outcome of following through on my end result was that I succeeded beyond my wildest expectation. It wasn't just that one of my dreams—exploring the exotic deserts of South West Africa—had come true. That was fantastic in itself, but so much more had come of it. The journey woke me up to the transformative power of the land in Africa. Someone once showed me a quote by some sociology professor who asserted that in every human being there is an existential angst that can only be resolved by standing on African soil. I now saw how true that was. The people who had come with me on safari were completely transformed by the experience, which had, without any structured or formal teaching, naturally facilitated a profound self-realization, connection to life, and sense of infinite possibility in them. In time, that very experience and awakening led me to taking, by now, close to a thousand people on safari through the enchanted southern end of the African Rift Valley, which to me is the most beautiful and effective way of introducing a human being to their *Genius*. In terms of professional outcome there's even more to it than that. That same original group later persuaded me to start running long-term Creative Development trainings. Not only did they constitute the nucleus of attendees of my first training, they also enthusiastically helped fill the training by enrolling their friends and family. As that Sufi saying goes: light doesn't travel, it unfolds out of itself. This book is a product of all that unfolded from that first safari in 1995.

Besides the benefit of cementing my vocational purpose in life, that experience bestowed on me an even greater gift. It helped heal my relationship with Africa and my family, with whom I now have the most joy-filled and inspired connection. That healing was effected not because I found the society different in any way, but because I discovered that the power to have life be the way that I would love it to be lies in how I choose it to be, not in the external conditions or circumstances I am confronted by. An unconscious society had never been my real problem with Africa; the problem had been my own sense of powerlessness.

A millennium ago, the Persian magician Assam observed, "In my experience, ninety eight percent of people use their minds to create poverty and misery, while only two percent use their minds to create fun and profit." I can relate very personally. By recognizing an end result I loved and following through on it, I definitely created an abundance of fun and profit, and by obstinately ignoring my *Super Conscious* wisdom and favoring my *Unconscious* rationalization, I sure did create a heap of poverty and misery for myself. If I had heeded my guidance and planned as if I was never returning to Australia, I would have let my townhouse and car go, sold my furniture, and stored my few possessions with Christian's family—and avoided the ongoing financial burden of rent and lease payments. Instead, I chose to interpret my guidance as meaning I had to live in Africa, an option that terrified me, truth be told. *Unconsciously*, my homeland evoked for me too strongly the sense of worthlessness and inferiority I imagined I had escaped by immigrating to Australia. Who knows, if I had taken the trouble to listen to my *Unconscious* fears, it is likely that I would have ceased to identify with them, and from there been open to my guidance. As a result, more clarity might have been revealed. But once my arrogance set in and I knew better than my guides, all channels to my *Super Conscious* had been cut off.

Rejecting my guidance wasn't the only point at which I kept myself on a *Low-Level Creative Frequency*. Because of my financial insecurity and, thereby, my investment in getting back to work, I willed my illness to be my hiatal hernia playing up and enrolled my doctors in agreeing with that diagnosis. Once again I didn't stop to listen to my fear-based *Unconscious* message, which inevitably led to unconscious behavior on my part. In retrospect I realize that I had emphasized the hiatal hernia symptoms and denied any inconsistent symptoms. I expect that if I had been open, and held an honest intention to discover my current reality, the doctors would have much sooner identified what was really wrong with me, and I might have been back on my feet in weeks rather than twelve months. As it happened, the stress of willing myself back to work ended up being a prolonged torture. Inevitably, I had to sort out all of my commitments and affairs from my sickbed. For someone in good health it wouldn't have been a big deal, but for me, in the condition I was in, it was a nightmare. And, on top of that, there was the struggle and ignominy of living on social welfare for a year, and a devastating collapse in the momentum of my new vocation.

I have no doubt that if I told this story to the average person, minus my self-responsible admissions, they would say that making the safari happen was a lucky break and that, when it came to being slammed by pericarditis, shit happens. But shit doesn't just happen. For those who have the awareness to observe human behavior with critical objectivity, they know that shit is created, and so is good luck. The outcomes we experience are purely a result of our focus, which means more than whether we manage to keep an unbroken line of sight with our goal or not. Actually it has more to do with which mode of awareness we pay attention to as we go for our goal.

THE IMPERATIVE OF FOLLOW-THROUGH

Now, I'd like to conclude this chapter by fulfilling my promise to you, which was that I'd explain why following through is so important. Let me correct myself: It's not important, it's imperative! It's not just that brilliant outcomes beyond your wildest imagination are going to unfold for you when you follow through. Nor is it because some terrible experience will necessarily result if you don't follow through. Nothing recognizably disastrous might happen. There is, however, a bigger picture being affected by your commitment or lack of it, which determines your level of creativity long-term and thereby your overall level of success in life. If you're serious about living your life on a *High-Level Creative Frequency*, which I'm sure you are, there are two things to consider: First of all, whether we are awake to it or not, our *Super Conscious* is constantly guiding us to our greatest possibility in life. That is the path of our personal destiny, and our truth is the light that illuminates the path. When we follow our truth we stick to our path and our destiny unfolds magnificently, an overall result far more fulfilling and satisfying than isolated achievements and experiences. Every time we don't follow our truth we step further away from our path, relegating ourselves to a second-best life in which we not only disconnect from our creative flow, but also miss out on the joy of expressing our highest nature and potential. Living life on a *High-Level Creative Frequency* is a thrill beyond compare.

More critical than anything, though, is the question of what message we give our *Subconscious* every time we follow our truth or don't. Don't forget that the ultimate determinant of what we experience in life is what we give the power to in our consciousness. Essentially there are two forces at play in our consciousness: our truth and our resistance to acting on our truth. Our resistance is born of our limiting beliefs, which hold that the conditions needed for actualizing our truth are absent—we don't have enough approval, or belonging, or accomplishment, or authority, or certainty, or permission, or power, or resources, or safety, or control, or knowledge, or whatever. When we don't follow through on our truth, regardless of how consequential or inconsequential we deem it to be, it's a function of our resistance and not the justifications we come up with to ease our conscience. When we capitulate to our resistance, we give our *Subconscious* the message that our beliefs have the power. That not only reinforces our beliefs, it also perpetuates a reality consistent with the beliefs.

But wait, there's more! Because the *Subconscious* concludes that the *Unconscious* has the power, it will also turn up the volume of the *Unconscious* messages and turn down the volume of the *Super Conscious* messages. Not being true to yourself damns you to a *Low-Level Creative Frequency*, which you then likely assume to be your inherent aptitude. But really what is going on is that your creative nonchalance has set up a structure—a groove—in which your *Genius* can't get through to you. Of course, developing a value of acting on your truth is going to have the reverse effect: your *Unconscious* is going to get turned down and you'll be subject to its influences less and less and, obviously, more and more aware of *Super Conscious* input.

Follow-through is vital on so many levels, as we've discussed. Without it you can't maintain yourself on a *High-Level Creative Frequency*, and if you're not on a *High-Level Creative Frequency*, you're not going to enjoy a consistent flow of *Natural Success*. In the next chapter, *Using the Emotion of the True End Result*, I'm going to teach you powerful techniques for creating end results of your choice, including psychological structures that make it more effortless and inevitable for you to take effective action and, by doing so, fulfill your *Self Conscious* role in your creations. I think you're going to really enjoy reading it.

CHAPTER FIVE
THE FIFTH STEP OF NATURAL SUCCESS

USING THE EMOTION OF THE TRUE END RESULT

Every night of my life, until I was thirty-eight, I lived through the same waking nightmare. I would go to sleep without any difficulty, and then inevitably wake up to the sound of someone breaking into my home. I could hear the rustle of their clothing as they came down the passage, or the staircase creaking as they climbed the stairs. In my mind I was certain of one thing: the intruder was coming to kill me. As I lay in bed holding my breath, my eyes wide with fright, I could hear the doorknob turning. Minutes would go by as I waited in abject terror for the killer to enter the room. I imagined I could see the door opening a crack. But the door never opened fully and no one ever came in. As if it was a pre-recorded scene, the sequence would replay itself all over again, starting with the sound of forced entry. There was nothing I could do to reassure myself that it was all in my imagination, that it wasn't rationally plausible for someone to be breaking in over and over every ten minutes or so. I did all kinds of therapy, but nothing helped. If I was home in Africa I slept with my pump-action shotgun beside me, and in Australia, where I couldn't own a gun, I kept a baseball bat beside my bed. Neither weapon made me feel any safer. In fact, the prospect of having to use them only heightened my anxiety.

Looking back, the origin of my paranoid delusion is obvious to me. Around the time I was six years old, pretty much the whole of Sub-Saharan Africa was consumed by *Uhuru*, the black uprising against white colonial rule. In some countries, like Kenya, it was a full-scale revolution. The Mau Mau were on the rampage butchering European settlers with impunity. For colonials, the most chilling part of the uprising was that house servants were enlisted to kill their own masters. Cooks and maids and gardeners who could not bring themselves to murder the families they had been a part of for years, and in some cases generations, hacked up the families on the neighboring estates, and their counterparts from those farms reciprocated by slaughtering their masters. The whites could barricade their houses and arm themselves to the teeth, but their executioners were embedded inside the sanctity of their fortress homes.

Uhuru rippled all the way down the continent. Though by the time it reached Swaziland, where we lived, it was a much more diluted affair. The peace-loving Swazis couldn't bring themselves to go past organizing a national strike. The British Army was brought in to break up the strike and keep an eye on the restless natives. Things were relatively under control in our neck of the woods, but that didn't stop the nervous chatter among the edgy white population about the state of affairs in the rest of the colonies. Speculation was rife about when the violence would flare up in our own territory. Hardly a day went by that I didn't hear the adults around me fretting over the horrifying possibility.

Using the Emotion of the True End Result

One hot summer night, around midnight, four shots rang out from the direction of our neighbor's house. My father heard the shots, but he didn't think anything of it. It was normal for the European farm managers billeted in the row of houses we lived in to shoot whichever animals came at night to graze on their vegetable gardens. It was such a familiar occurrence that we could tell who was shooting by the sound of the rifle fire. In the morning, just before sunrise, my siblings and I were in bed with my parents having a snuggle, as was our family custom, when our neighbor's cook arrived at our house in a highly agitated state, insisting that my father come with him. When asked what the problem was, the weeping servant would not say; he only implored my father to follow him with the utmost haste. When they arrived at our neighbor's home, the cook led my father into the master bedroom, where the most appalling sight greeted him. Our field manager and his wife lay dead in bed, both with gunshot wounds in the head and chest. Clinging to them silently were their three children, the one boy my age and two younger ones.

The murderer was apprehended within days. It turned out to be Lettuce, our neighbor's former gardener, who not long before had been jailed for stealing money from them. He'd made an easy escape from the low-security prison they had put him in and headed straight back to our farm, fully resolved to exact revenge on his ex-employer. On the way, he broke into a house in town and stole some money and a handgun. A couple of nights later, he walked through our neighbor's unlocked front door and used the revolver to fulfill his mission. Straight after that he began turning up at local shebeens—the African version of a speakeasy—where he bragged about his deed and bought everyone home-brewed liquor. The police soon got wind of the killer's activities and staked out the shebeens he had been visiting. Much to the relief of every white person in the country, he was arrested, tried, and sentenced to death by hanging.

Everyone on the farm was shocked by the tragic incident. We all remembered Lettuce as a sweet and gentle soul.

Whenever I visited the kids next door he used to pull carrots out of the ground and wash them off for us to eat. As it turned out, he had quite an aptitude for being an outlaw. Somehow he managed to escape from the maximum-security prison where he was waiting on death row. Once again he began appearing in shebeens, this time letting it be known that he was heading back to our farm to kill my family. A whole company of the Queen's Lancashire Regiment was dispatched to protect us. For the first time in our lives we locked our doors at night and both my mother and father slept with loaded pistols on their bedside tables. Every day brought reports of Lettuce sightings, all of them tracing a direct line in our direction. And then, after a sighting not far from us, he disappeared off the radar. For weeks there was no news of his whereabouts. Everyone waited anxiously for him to strike. It was like waiting for a circling shark to attack. In that period, the African drums we were used to hearing at night fell eerily silent. Our hunting dogs took to barking at their own shadows. All the talk among the whites was speculation about what Lettuce was up to and what his next move might be. Eventually he had a run-in with some soldiers guarding a river crossing five miles from our house. A massive manhunt ensued. Lettuce escaped across the border into Mozambique. As an unwelcome alien in that country he survived by robbing and killing. The Portuguese eventually caught him and executed him in short order. The story I heard was that the devoutly Catholic Portuguese, to absolve themselves of killing a condemned man by their own hands, kicked Lettuce from an army helicopter twenty miles out to sea, where his drowning could be categorized as death by natural causes.

The homicidal gardener might not have succeeded in killing my family, but nevertheless he did exact some kind of revenge on us for whatever he perceived we had done to hurt him and, maybe, his people. He would surely be happy to know that he had terrorized me every night of my life for thirty years. Of course, Lettuce wasn't solely responsible for my waking nightmares. One of the great fallacies, I believe, of many Personal Development and Spiritual Healing modalities is that we are wounded by a single trauma in our backgrounds. It is much more the case that a consistent pattern of experience counter to our well-being in early childhood is responsible for establishing our limiting beliefs, which then attract the outstanding events we see as the source of our existential problems. When my mother was pregnant with me, my father sent her to get an abortion. As it happened, the doctor friend she went to harshly declined, and not only that, told my mother to tell my father that if their unborn baby did not survive to be a healthy child, he would have them charged with murder. Despite the doctor's merciful intervention, as far back as I remember, I had the uneasy sense that some malevolent force in the universe was coming for me, like a knitting needle invading the sanctity of my mother's womb. That terrifying time, in the midst of Uhuru, waiting for Lettuce to break through the protective military shield around my family and take us out no doubt reinforced my inherent sense of mortal vulnerability.

The time came, though, when I couldn't stand the torture another night. It was while I was waiting for Christian to return from Europe and come to live with me that I decided to face my demon stalker. One night before I went to bed, I threw my baseball bat out the window and lay naked on my bed, leaving the bedroom door wide open. Inevitably the phantom intruder appeared. I felt the usual horror invade my heart. But this time, rather than cringe helplessly, I willed my imaginary nemesis to come and finish me. I even called out, "I'm in here, you cunt. Come and get me." When the dark shadow of my executioner fell across the threshold of the doorway into my room, instead of freezing in terror, I breathed into my impending death, only hoping that it would be quick. This dreadful experience kept up for three nights, and then, after that, it was over. I never died, and that waking nightmare never visited me again. And while that lifelong sense of unviability (like I'm a crab without a shell) still haunts me at times, it is a much more watered-down dynamic that I am now able to use my will to rise above.

We are all haunted by demons, whether consciously or unconsciously. And until we face our demons they will keep chasing us in the opposite direction of our true-life path, forever denying us the fulfillment born of being who we really are and creating what really matters to us. In the late 1980s, the *Greed is Good* era, my good friend, author and best-selling financial journalist Ruth Ostrow wrote a book on the mega-successful immigrants in Australia. These were people from Chinese, Jewish, Italian, Greek, Lebanese and other backgrounds who had generally suffered great persecution or poverty in their countries of origin. Many had escaped World War 11 only to be interned as enemies when they arrived. There were survivors from the Holocaust, and those who had endured racial vilification, displacement or severe paucity. They came to the Great Southern Land, seeking freedom and success. Motivated by the insecurity of their pasts many worked arduously as entrepreneurs and amassed huge fortunes—becoming billionaires by today's standards. But despite their lavish or distinguished lives, most were still driven by their existential insecurity, never feeling safe no matter how much money they made or how prominent they became. Some worked themselves to an early grave or breakdown, several of them were jailed for corporate crimes. Many lost it all taking one gamble too many. All no doubt driven by an insatiable bid to cover up their deep-seated feelings of powerlessness. It is no small irony that, for some, the quest for freedom that extreme wealth and power can often buy, led to their becoming the very prisoners - of the State, of their unwell bodies and tormented minds - that they most feared.

We can sneer and tut-tut at the misguided values of these megalomaniac businessmen, but we are all subject to the same *Compensating Tendency* as they were, albeit mostly at a less intense and obvious level. We all have limiting beliefs that hold that we are unviable in some way, and *Unconsciously* we assume that the meaning of our lives is to make ourselves viable so we can resolve our beliefs. Neale Donald Walsch, the author of *Conversations with God*, once said that ninety-eight percent of all human activity is a waste of energy. The truth of that startling statement lies in the fact that mostly what people are up to in life is trying to be the opposite of who they fear they are. By default, we all believe that we can only create what we love once we have rectified the conditions we imagine preclude our viability. Inevitably what most people strive for in life is compelled by whatever they feel incomplete about. The problem being, of course, that they are not ever really going for anything so much as trying to get away from something. That is what I call a *Negative Vision*.

What you resist will always persist as aggressively as you resist it. No matter how much you defy your beliefs, if they are driving what you want to create, your *Subconscious* has to assume they have the power in your consciousness. Your *Compensating Tendency* will inevitably perpetuate perceptions and experiences consistent with your *Unconscious* worldview. All of your suffering and struggle in life is a direct result of this dysfunctional dynamic. When you are subject to a reactive orientation in life, success will only ever mean masking your fears satisfactorily. True success—expressing your sovereign nature and having your life be the way you would really love it to be—will always elude you.

A long time ago now, I was given a big, thick book on comparative religion for my birthday. It catalogued the main spiritual themes common to all religions throughout history and what each of them had to say about the different subjects. I was intrigued that the most universal theme the compilers of the anthology had found was the principle *"Know thyself,"* which I had only ever associated with the Oracle at Delphi. To me, it makes sense that of all the spiritual ideals espoused, *knowing thyself* should be the most pervasive. After all, if we are not intimately aware of our own temperaments and tendencies, and what aspects of our consciousness they serve, how can we ever know whether we are functionally engaged with end results that are true for us or not?

When it comes to establishing a vision relating to some aspect of your life, or making decisions as you progress towards your desired end results, the more acquainted you are with yourself and your dynamics, the better you will be at separating your *Compensating Tendencies* from your *High-Level Creative Process*. I referred earlier to the Sufi saying that the dysfunctional personality is the gateway to the soul, which at its deepest level I take to mean that, as human beings, we are inescapably anchored in the reality of our *Unconscious Beliefs*, and that only through a deep appreciation of our humanness can we transcend that reality. One way we can learn about ourselves is through the act of creating. Whenever we go for our dreams, anything in our consciousness that doesn't trust that we're ready to go for them will come up to tell us so, giving us the perfect opportunity to go through the *Conflict Deconstruction Exercise* and uncover what we believe about ourselves, others, and life, and what we're giving the power to in our consciousness. But aside from the self-awareness you gain from your creative process, it is also helpful to have a more generalized overview of your own personality and the foibles your personality type is prone to. Therefore, we're going to look at that, and I think you're going to find the exercise quite fascinating.

We all have distinct personalities, distinguished by consistent behavioral characteristics. While we might all appear to be very diverse individuals, when we boil our personalities down, it is amazing how neatly they fit into one or another of a handful of distinct types. When you begin to understand human nature, you realize that, although there are billions of us on Planet Earth, our personalities are formed from a very limited set of psychological molds. Twelve or less, depending on which model of personality typing you subscribe to.

PERSONALITY TYPES

According to the *Natural Success* premise, personality is a defense against identity. Your identity is formed by the *Fundamental Beliefs* you take on in the *Individuation Phase*. They form the foundation for the limiting definitions of self, others, and the world that you identify with. Your *Egoic* instinct is to resolve your identity, to make up for your sense of incompleteness. The predictable strategies you develop to compensate for your particular sense of incompleteness—the way in which you pay attention, the perceptions that arise from that focus, and the behavior you use to deal with your reality—restrict you to a narrow set of traits you share with everyone else holding the same beliefs as you. A broad overview of personality types can help you identify your own *Low-Level Creative* characteristics—again, those characteristics that dominate and define your personality when you are coming from the perception of your incompleteness—which in turn can help you disassociate from the dysfunctional matrix you inhabit psychologically. The more you can recognize and see through your *Egoic* illusion when it is in play, the easier it is to begin *Self Consciously* shifting to identifying with your *Super Conscious* truth.

The personality typing model I use in my trainings is the Enneagram. In Greek, *enneagram* means "nine points." This system defines nine distinct types. It's an intriguing model, developed at least two thousand five hundred years ago (some evidence suggests five thousand years ago) in Sumer, now modern-day Iraq. One has to marvel at what kind of *Genius* devised this sophisticated typology way back in the Bronze Age. It is represented by the points of a geometric chart (see diagram overleaf), which also indicate intricate connections between the types. Although modern practitioners of the system have named each type based on their essential disposition, traditionally each type was designated only by its number. While each number is assigned to a core personality type, that number reverts in low stress to the disposition of the preceding number in the chart, and in high stress advances to the disposition of the superseding number. On top of that, each number has a wing, or wings, depending on which Enneagram school you belong to (personally, I lean more to the one-wing premise, but not religiously), meaning that it also draws on the numbers to either side of it. As an example, number 2 will come from 4 in low stress and go to 8 in high stress. It will also, at times, incorporate the characteristics of its 1 or 3 wings.

As if the low stress and high stress numbers and wings aren't intricate enough, each number belongs to one of three groups, each of which is rooted in particular aspects of the human psyche. Numbers 2, 3, and 4 are emotionally centered and depression based; 5, 6, and 7 are mentally centered and fear based; 8, 9, and 1 are instinctively centered and anger based. Further, looking at the Enneagram diagram, you'll notice that numbers 3, 6, and 9 are on their own triangular axis, each of them at the center of their own groupings. Fascinatingly, while they are the core numbers of their particular groupings, they relate to their aspects of psyche by virtue of denial. Number 3s repress their emotions, especially depression; 6s deny their intellect and fear; and 9s deny their instinct and anger. Also, because of the way the numbers are grouped, you will notice that the majority of Enneagram models list their types starting with 2 and finishing with 1.

Using the Emotion of the True End Result

Film : Pleasantville

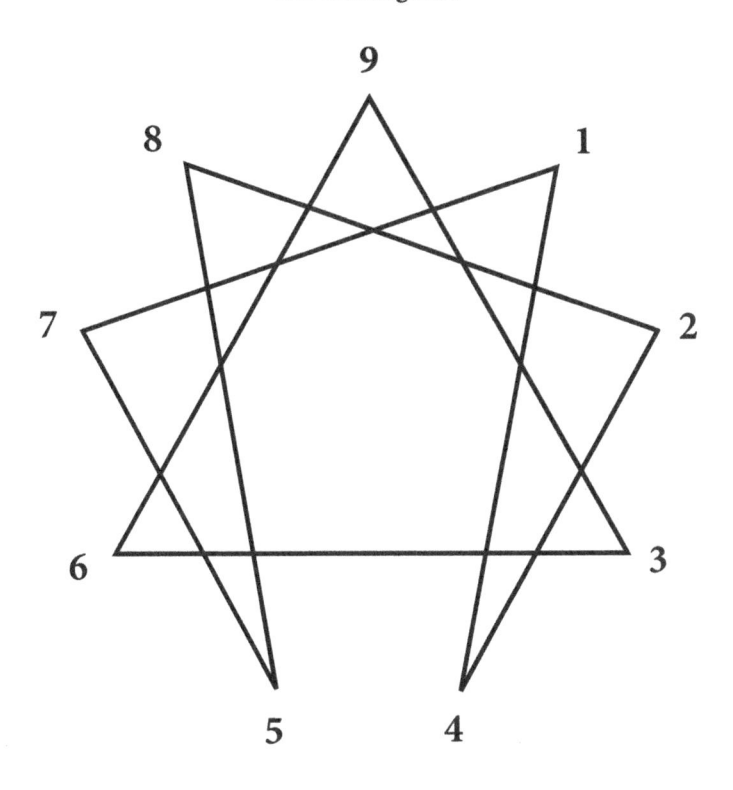

The Enneagram

```
        9
    8       1
  7           2
    6       3
      5   4
```

You couldn't put a puzzle as complex as the Enneagram together rationally. I'm convinced it could only have been *Super Consciously* conceived, which is one of the reasons I am in awe of the typology. It also happens to provide deep clarity and insight into the different types, as well as demonstrate remarkable structural integrity (as an example of how well the types relate to each other, number 2—the Helper—is a very pleasant type who goes to the super-aggressive number 8—the Boss—in high stress, when their helpful, approval-seeking ways fail to get them what they want; this impeccable cause-and-effect dynamic flows through the whole system). Mostly, I favor the Enneagram above any other systems I've come across because of how well it fits in with the core principles of my *Natural Success* model. Each type's worldview, disposition, and behavioral characteristics are so obviously the product of one, and in a few cases two, of the *Fundamental Beliefs*.

Self-awareness is crucial when it comes to shifting from *Low-Level Creative Function* to *High-Level Creative Function*. The more familiar you are with the nature of your *Unconscious*, the better you will be at recognizing its influence on you. As a gateway to exploring the shadow side of your personality, I highly recommend that you familiarize yourself with this time-tested system. While it is not the scope of this chapter to explain the Enneagram system or describe the personalities in too much detail—there are a lot of good books that do that already—I do want to help you understand the psychological foundation of each type in terms of their worldview, the *Compensating Strategies* promoted by the worldview, and also the most fundamental character traits those strategies give rise to. Not only will this give you a fundamental understanding of the system and the types themselves, you likely won't find this *"belief seeking resolution"* explanation of Enneagram types anywhere else. Because each personality type arises out of a particular belief system, reviewing the twelve *Fundamental Beliefs* and their strategies and behaviors in Chapter Two will help you understand and recognize the types even more clearly.

NUMBER 2: THE HELPER

Core Belief: "I'm not worthy."

Assumption: Can't express or go for what they want because they are not worthy. Once they've done enough to be good then they will be given what *they* want.

Compensating Strategies: Being a good person. Helping and putting others first.

Personality Profile: Caring, sociable person who behaves how they assume others want them to (they are sometimes known as chameleons). Find it difficult to know their own mind. Possessive. Manipulative (because they help others in the unconscious expectation that it will lead to them being given what they want). Have a nasty streak, which reveals itself when their hidden agenda fails to bear fruit.

NUMBER 3: THE ACHIEVER

Core Belief: "I'm not good enough."

Assumption: That if they achieve enough they will be valid.

Compensating Strategies: Seek to accomplish a lot, learn a lot.

Personality Profile: Competitive, self-promoting, over-achieving, workaholic, perpetual student. Pragmatic and adaptive. Someone who identifies strongly with achievement and the image of success.

NUMBER 4: THE TRAGIC ROMANTIC

Core Belief: "I don't belong."

Assumption: That there is something about them that makes them unlovable. All 4s were abandoned in childhood, either literally or effectively.

Compensating Strategies: Either seek to fit in or be odd as a pre-emptive strike to being rejected, be attractive enough to be loved, find out or cover up what's wrong with them.

Personality Profile: Sensitive, dramatic, self-absorbed, temperamental, and given to melancholy; one type presents as odd and eccentric, another type presents as icy cool and stylish; artistic, expressive.

NUMBER 5: THE THINKER

Core Belief: "I need to control myself/my space."

Assumption: That if they are open, their boundaries will be violated.

Compensating Strategies: Be aloof. Protect themselves by living mentally.

Personality Profile: Intensely cerebral, observant, innovative, aloof, deny their own needs (because if they have needs they can't maintain their aloofness).

NUMBER 6: THE LOYALIST/TERRORIST

Core Belief: "I'm not safe." (Trust)

Assumption: Only safe with protection of an authority (loyalist) or in the absence of authority (terrorist).

Compensating Strategies: There are actually two types of 6s. One is very loyal (phobic) and the other is confrontational (counter-phobic) in relation to authority. Always testing safety.

Personality Profile: Both types are anxious and suspicious. Engaging, responsible, timid, and ingratiating if a phobic 6 (loyalist). Abrasive, aggressive contrarian if a counter-phobic 6 (terrorist).

DENIES: Their own authority

NUMBER 7: THE EPICURE

Core Belief: "I don't have the capacity. There is *a* way."

Assumption: That there is a way they should be and if they get it wrong they'll be in trouble...and that they don't know the way to be.

Compensating Strategies: Develop many interests. Enroll others in how great everything they do is. Try to prove they've got "it."

Personality Profile: Effervescent optimists with insatiable appetite for life. Busy, fun-loving, spontaneous, and versatile. Trying out everything but committing to nothing.

DENIES: Commitment + negativity

NUMBER 8: THE BOSS

Core Belief: "I'm powerless."

Assumption: That if they don't dominate, they'll be dominated. Only the dominant get what they want.

Compensating Strategies: Strive to be in a position of power. Align self with powerful others. Preoccupation with power and control.

Personality Profile: Willful, dominating, confrontational, overtly angry, combative.

NUMBER 9: THE PEACEMAKER

Core Belief: "I'm ~~powerless~~. I'm not allowed to be capable." *["I'm not allowed to be powerful"]*

Assumption: That if conflict or tension is present they won't get what they want. That expressing what they want creates conflict or tension, so to get what they want they mustn't let on that they want it.

Compensating Strategies: Avoid conflict, tension, and knowing their own direction. Don't take much action. Fill up their time with inessential activity.

Personality Profile: Easygoing, receptive, reassuring, agreeable. Self-effacing, often shy and retiring, even withdrawn (can be confused with number 5 in that sense). Attracted to peaceful environments and endeavors. Decidedly unambitious. Dreamer. Passive-aggressive.

NUMBER 1: THE PERFECTIONIST

Core Belief: "I need to be perfect. There is a right way."

Assumption: That perfection actually exists and they would need to be perfect before they could create what they want.

Compensating Strategies: Avoid doing things unless they can be done perfectly. Avoid criticism by being perfect, defensive, or deflecting criticism on to something or someone else.

Personality Profile: Principled, self-controlled, self-righteous, judgmental, and critical type, keen for themselves to be seen as perfect. Share the 9's idealism and desire for peace, relief, and resolution and the 2's penchant for approval and being good. Strongly reject their Dark Side.

THE DARK SIDE OF PERSONALITY TYPING

It is more than interesting to note that Gurdjieff, the charismatic mystic who learned the Enneagram from the Sufi brotherhoods of Southern Asia and later brought it to the West, didn't believe that Westerners were ready for the typology. He never taught the system to his students overtly, preferring instead to transfer it energetically through a graceful dance that choreographed the nine-pointed diagram and the relationships between the numbers. The Sufis, who did not devise the Enneagram but were its custodians for the last one thousand years, were clear that our personality is only the mask we wear on top of who we are, not who we really are. The benefit of a personality typing system like the Enneagram is that, by making us aware of our fixed wounded preoccupations and behavioral strategies, it potentially enables us to let go of that limited, reactive way of being in the world and develop a more creative worldview and response to life.

The most *unhelpful* relationship we can have with the Enneagram—or any other system, like astrology, for example—is to assume that our personalities explain who we are absolutely and the extent of our potential. Gurdjieff must have known that we in the West, with our mechanical understanding of ourselves and fixing orientation, would gleefully seize on the Enneagram to help us with putting ourselves and each other in neat little boxes. Hence, obviously, his reluctance to pass on a phenomenal tool that we would only use to concretize our *Egoic* identities, rather than move on to our unlimited potential.

Most Enneagram books I have read do a good job in explaining the system and describing the traits of the different numbers. Where some of them fall down, in my opinion, is when they relate to the types based on the assumption that a human being is only the sum of their type and nothing more. Really, it doesn't help anyone to be reassured or encouraged in their so-called positive characteristics when those characteristics may well be compensating for a limiting belief. For instance, being helpful is unarguably a noble quality, generally speaking, but as an indiscriminate reaction designed to resolve one's *Unconscious* sense of worthlessness, compulsive helping will only lead to giving yourself away and reinforcing your sense of worthlessness. The true benefit of knowing that you are an addictive savior allows you to desist from that compulsion and become *Super Consciously* aware of the most empowered response in individual situations.

If you truly believe in the infinite potential of *Genius*, and that it exists in all of us, you will also see the glaring limitation in the proposition that a person's life purpose is to become the positive opposite of their dysfunctional type. The quest to become a better person is a reasonable aspiration, but the invisible motivation underlying such a quest is all too often the *Unconscious* notion that there is something inherently wrong with us and that we need to fix ourselves (and, by the same logic, everyone else) before we can experience life as we would love it to be. In fact, the quest to fix ourselves only serves in doing just that—fixing us to our identities, which in the first place formed our personalities.

Don't let anyone kid you. There is no higher side to personality. Or to put it another way, the higher side of personality is *Genius*—and *Genius* doesn't come in any set mold. Anyone who proposes that there is some standard ideal that you should strive for based on your personality is damning you to a misguided preoccupation with your *Egoic* identity, and thereby a *Low-Level Creative Frequency*. And anyone who proposes that your *Genius* has a set nature with set characteristics, gifts, and abilities, as an extension of your personality, is someone still identified with the mechanical illusion of *Egoic* identity, who hasn't seen beyond the human mask to eternity, where our unique, sovereign, and splendid *Genius* awaits us.

USING THE HIGHER AGAINST THE LOWER

Nowhere will you find a more unequivocal or dynamic premise relating to the transcendence of the *Egoic* illusion than in Alchemy. Let us for a moment consider the extraordinary *Hermetic Law of Vibration,* which holds that everything in the universe, visible or invisible, is essentially pure energy or light resonating at a particular vibratory frequency. This principle was not so long ago laughable according to our material understanding of the world, but it now corresponds with the latest scientific discoveries indicating that matter is in fact more ray-like in nature than the solid form we perceive it as. And yet, the philosophers of Ancient Egypt and Greece put this Hermetic principle forward thousands of years ago. Further to this principle, the philosophers also proposed that every vibration in the universe exists in our consciousness. To some students of metaphysics, this explains our psychic ability. How else could we know everything through all time and space, they reason, if it doesn't exist as part of who we are?

While we may find the *Law of Vibration* intriguing, on its own it's not much more than a far-out concept. Its real benefit to us as creators lies in the related *Hermetic Law of Polarity,* which holds that everything is on the same vibration as its opposite, just at different ends of the spectrum. If you remember the old mercury thermometer, which was used to take someone's temperature, the instrument registered hot and cold as higher and lower degrees on the same scale; they were not measured by separate instruments. So too, then, can we think of good and bad as higher and lower degrees on the scale of worth, or rich and poor as higher and lower degrees on the scale of wealth, or well and ill as higher and lower degrees on the scale of health, and so on.

Using the Emotion of the True End Result

Vibrational Polarity

Good .... Bad
Worth

Hot .... Cold
Temperature

Rich .... Poor
Wealth

Well .... Sick
Health

According to this principle, our identities are formed by our *Unconsciously* fixing ourselves at arbitrary points on all the different vibrations in our consciousness. The *Natural Success* premise assumes this takes place during the *Individuation Phase* when we decide where on the scale of worth or capability or power or safety or intelligence or creativity, etc., we are or belong. Where we place ourselves on the various vibrations then gives us a sense of who we are. Our orientation—where we come from in life—is then determined by our *Egoic* tension to compensate for our identities, which we have roundly seen only perpetuates our *Unconscious* sense of self.

Here we need to pay close attention to the Hermetic axiom of *using the higher against the lower*. This is a very important principle of Alchemy, and anyone who doesn't understand it or heed it isn't going to create much gold in their life. What it means is that you can't rise to the higher end of any vibration by working on that vibration itself. In other words, you can't escape poverty by striving for abundance, especially if you're striving against poverty. That's only going to put the power into where you're fixed on the vibration of wealth. To really unfix yourself from any point on any vibration, you have to let it go—stop trying to fix it—and work on a higher level in the hierarchy of vibration. I have noticed, for example, many people's fortunes change from scarcity to abundance once they stop battling financial insecurity and allow themselves to become unconditionally involved in their life purpose.

A powerful example of using the higher against the lower can be found in drug and alcohol recovery, of which I have some experience. Alcoholics and drug addicts who have tried everything to stop their substance abuse without success give up their habits relatively easily when they stop fighting their addictions and dedicate themselves to a spiritual practice, which includes being of service within their fellowships. By their own testimonies, they go from being depraved, shattered souls to becoming wholesome individuals. It is very telling that trying to change their behavior neither leads addicts and alcoholics to a change in behavior or to living functional, worthwhile lives. But dedicating themselves to a higher principle naturally achieves both.

As I pointed out right at the beginning of this book, success and failure are structural, not personal. While the addict or alcoholic is in the grip of their so-called disease, they experience themselves as utterly powerless, battling the whole world, which is apparently against them. Though they can't see it themselves, their struggle and suffering is entirely a result of their *Unconsciously* fighting their own inner demons, all the while giving those demons more and more power. Yet, when they surrender, when they effectively give up the battle and focus on a principle aligned with their own spirit, they correct back onto a path flowing gracefully in line with their higher potential. Once they are in this higher structure, they no longer feel powerless or at odds with the world. Just the opposite—they feel themselves supported and guided by what they call their *Higher Power*, what we would call our *Super Conscious* or *Genius*. This *Grace*—which is a word frequently used in recovery—is a principle central to *Natural Success*.

TRANSCENDENCE

If success and failure are structural, then it makes sense to set up *Self Conscious* structures that naturally lead us to living life as an expression of our higher potential. I know people who tell me that they don't like structure, that they like to go with the flow. Well, guess what? We are all subject to structure whether we like it or not. It's just a question of whether you want to be subject to structures that perpetuate your living and operating on a *Low-Level Creative Frequency* or whether you're prepared to use your *Will* to set up structures that will elevate you to a more brilliant experience of yourself and life.

Structure is defined as two or more points with a relationship to each other. In terms of consciousness, structure is determined by where we are—the point we're at—and what we're focused on—the point we're headed to. By default, our structures are mostly *Unconscious* and reflect our *Compensating Logic*, our compulsion to resolve our sense of incompleteness. The point the *Ego* always strives towards is meeting the conditions it believes will satisfy its survival. Like the gold-hoarding dragons of mythology, it only uses its energy to protect our identity, never to create anything new.

When I do visioning exercises in my trainings, designed to establish what participants would love to create in their lives, I first ask the participants to write down what they *Self Consciously* assume they would love to manifest. Next, I get them to write down all the ways in which they feel incomplete. Finally, I ask them to compare the two lists. Invariably, almost their entire list of what they want is exactly a mirror opposite of their inner sense of lack. A set of rationally formulated goals or *Choices*, as I call them, regardless of an individual's level of creative mastery, will invariably reflect their *Unconscious* drive to resolve their limited beliefs. If you've been following me so far, there should be no need for me to explain the drawbacks of a direction in life dictated by your *Have Not* nature. No matter how proficient you are at fulfilling your *Negative Vision*, you will only ever be perpetuating your *Low-Level Creative* condition, thereby eternally denying yourself the grace-filled creative power that is your birthright.

Transcending our identity doesn't require that we resolve it by denying, fixing, or obliterating it. That would assume it has the power in our consciousness and, in fact, just give it more power. We only need to set up a higher structure by hooking into the end results that are true for us to create—end results that are free of our *Compensating Logic* and express what really matters to us. We all have a true nature that seeks to be freely expressed in life, and gifts, abilities, and talents that support that expression. Our higher purpose is to claim that nature and use those inherent qualities to become all that we can be. There, within that nature and purpose, lies our *Genius*, and nowhere else. And the most powerful way that we can activate and sustain our *Genius* is by creating a foundation that supports it in flourishing.

CHOICES AND THE EMOTION OF THE TRUE END RESULT

Earlier in the book, we established the premise that our *Subconscious* creates our reality based on the messages it gets and, based on those messages, where it assumes the power is. *Will* is the mechanism by which we assign the power in our consciousness. *Choice* is the *Self Conscious* formalization of *Will*. To anyone intending to live their life on a *High-Level Creative Frequency*, I have to say: START MAKING SUPER CONSCIOUSLY FORMULATED CHOICES!

I don't only advocate that you make *Super Consciously Formulated Choices* so that you can create great things in your life. You will do that. Once you start making *Choices* you're not only going to manifest end results beyond your wildest dreams, you're also going to experience the joy of waking up to and applying gifts and talents and powers you never even imagined existed in anyone, let alone yourself. But beyond the thrill of unleashing your *Creative Spirit*, making true *Choices* has two very important additional benefits: it anchors you in a *High-Level Creative Structure*, and it attunes you to your *Genius*-level emotions. Once these two dynamics come into play, you're suddenly going to wonder where the wings you're flying around on sprouted from!

In the Bible, Christ is quoted as saying, "No one can see the kingdom of God unless they are born again." Those who take this to mean that one has to be baptized into the Christian Church are welcome to their interpretation. To me, the kingdom of God is a reference to *Higher Consciousness*, the exalted condition we connect with through our own *Genius*. If you think about it, you can't be born again unless you first die. And it's equally true that you can't embody your own *Genius* while you're still stuck in your identity. To move on from your fears and desires and pass through to eternity, as Dante put it, you have to die to the wounded persona you took on when you first got here and wake up to your eternal nature.

Indigenous initiation was designed to facilitate this transformation from the infantile identity to the fully formed human, who, by the way, is one with all of existence. In *Iron John*, the brilliant treatise on manhood, Robert Bly identifies three universal themes in male initiation: the wound, the being within, and everything is conscious. If the collective indigenous wisdom of the ages is anything to go by, then it is universally agreed that within us exists an essential nature connected to everything through time and space that through our wounding we unavoidably become separated from. Initiation serves the individual in being restored to their true nature. It fulfills the function of true education, if you will.

It's too bad that modern society has lost sight of human *Genius,* and that it considers the rituals that serve its members in being born again as primitive irrelevances. But it actually doesn't matter that we have not been served by our society with a true education or a functional initiation.

We can fulfill that function for ourselves by understanding the nature of consciousness and beginning to act in favor of our higher nature. That is exactly what we do when we die to our *Compensating Logic* and start making *Super Consciously Directed Choices*.

Which brings us to the part that's going to knock your socks off. Not long ago I was watching Tony Robbins's TED Talk. It's mandatory viewing, I have to say. In his audience are some of the most highly accomplished people of our time, including Al Gore, former Vice President of the United States, who won an Oscar for his documentary, *An Inconvenient Truth*. Robbins asks his esteemed audience to raise their hands if they can admit to failures in their lives. Everyone's hand goes up. Next, Robbins asks the roomful of high achievers to cite what lack of resources they blame for their failures. As each reason is called out it lights up on the screen behind the super-coach: didn't have the technology, didn't have enough knowledge, and, surprisingly for a roomful of multimillionaires, didn't have enough time and money. A moment of humor ensues, as Al Gore nominates not having the Supreme Court in his pocket as the reason he lost the 2000 presidential election to George W. Bush. As the powerful creators that they are, the audience, along with Al Gore, has no problem in agreeing with Robbins that all the given reasons are merely excuses, and not the honest cause of their failures. What might have been news to some or all of them is the true determinant that Robbins reveals—the emotion underlying the pursuit of end results. The perfect case in point he uses is the lack of passion Al Gore evidenced in his election campaign, which, had it been present, would have easily garnered him enough votes to win the election without the Supreme Court being forced to weigh in on the outcome.

We already know from the story of Wag Dodge and the escape fire that emotions drive decisions and actions, which constitute behavior. While we might be mystified by—or even have all kinds of theories for—the way things work out in our lives, our behavior is the cause of all the effects we generally experience. Knowing this gives you the ultimate key to creative mastery, especially when you consider the fact that every choice you make is loaded with the emotion of its motivating principle.

When you are driven by the tension to resolve your limited beliefs, the emotion corresponding with those beliefs pervades your consciousness, promoting stale thinking and strategies. In the structure of *Negative Vision*, you will always be struggling against your sense of separation and limitation, forever having to force your way through the fears, doubts, and obstacles the underlying emotion impresses on you. For instance, if your ambition for high achievement is motivated by your sense of *I'm Not Good Enough*, the emotion of emptiness will resound in your *Subconscious*, even while on the surface you might feel highly enthused. End results will be attained more by hard, mechanical work than as a result of creative flow. And when you finally do get your outcome, you may feel disappointed that it is not as satisfying as you anticipated...somehow, it is meaningless, not enough. Certainly Tony Robbins's TED Talk audience could relate to this last point.

On the other hand, when your vision is true, and your end result is born of what you honestly love, that aspiration is aligned with your *Genius*, the part of you connected to everything through all time and space. The corresponding emotion will carry the resonance of your most inspired level of consciousness. Here, I'll just say that this *Super Conscious* type of emotion is not of the same quality as those we associate with *Unconscious* reaction, like anger or fear or shame—not even the so-called positive reactions like excitement, elation, and cheerfulness. It has a more refined resonance, an almost empty and serene quality, yet unequivocally conveying a sense of connection to whatever you are relating to. This higher emotion induces creative insights and solutions, as well as enthuses you to take dynamic action. The sense of connection to your desired end result awakens you to its greater benefit and encourages you in its possibility, all of which energize you in following through. Under the influence of the *Emotion of*

True End Results, you are automatically more engaged, inspired, and proactive, all qualities highly beneficial to creating great outcomes in life.

The big difference between your reactive emotions and your creative emotions is that your reactive emotions are heavier and more palpable. Your creative emotions are lighter and less perceptible, and to feel them takes a *Self Conscious* effort. The best way of getting in touch with your creative emotions is by building and holding a vision of your *True End Results*. When I was writing *The Magician's Way*, I would visualize the qualities that I wanted the book to evoke, feel into the subtle emotions of those qualities, and then start writing. The words poured out of those emotions. As someone technically wholly unqualified to write, my only talent was to write down faithfully the words streaming through my consciousness. If ever I felt myself getting stuck, I'd just go back to the emotion, and the words would flow again. (Here's a tip to you writers out there: if you're experiencing writer's block, you're just separate from the emotion of your offering.) Yes, it takes a little effort to connect with the emotion of your *True End Result*, but by stopping short of this step, you are robbing yourself of the vast untapped creative energy permanently at your disposal.

CREATING YOUR GENIUS FOUNDATION

Oscar Wilde once said that all art is useless. What he presumably meant is that art is created purely for its own sake, not because it will lead to something else. The urge that produces it is nothing other than the artist's desire for self-expression. An artist may have a big *Ego*, but if they really are a creator, there is no *Ego* in their art. Living on a *High-Level Creative Frequency* is akin to creating your life as a work of art.

The mistake most people make is that their approach to life is one in which they try to satisfy all of the conditions they hope will lead to them being able to one day do what they really love. They hope that by establishing economic security, and getting set in a binding life partnership, and winning the approval of their society or peers, and generally attaining whatever they believe it takes to be whole, they will somehow find the fulfillment they are *Unconsciously* striving for. Of all the misguided misconceptions we are subject to, this is perhaps the most fatal. Preparing to live never leads to living—only more preparation. Despair and disappointment arise firstly from failing to secure the conditions we expect make us whole, and finally from the realization that the conditions aren't what satisfy us anyway. The only way that you can ever live the life you love *and* achieve the conditions that satisfy your viability is to start by living the life you love.

Personal power is the ability to clearly recognize, decide to have, go for, and manifest what you love—it is not the ability to accrue the symbols of power. Making *Choices* is the most basic expression of your power. Once you start making *Choices* you realize how little you made *Choices* before. You'll be surprised just how often, before you allow yourself to become fully conscious of what you'd love in any situation or even long term, you bury your true preference with considerations of how you'd be able to get it and whether you'd be safe going for it or having it—to the point that you end up halfhearted about what you love or not interested in it at all. You tend to give resources like knowledge, confidence, time, money, certainty, your own capacity, and others' approval and acceptance the power. Any setback, real or imagined, only confirms the scarcity of those resources and the unlikelihood of you having what you want. In your lifetime you learned to expect and hope and wish a lot, but your education failed to train you in being powerful, especially in your ability to *Self Consciously* choose for yourself.

When making *Choices*, especially major life goals and decisions that lead directly to you living the life you love and doing and having what really matters to you, the capacity for *Vision* is absolutely essential. *Vision*, as I use it here, is the ability to see beyond the limits of your current understanding and experience to the highest possibility of anything. It is, quite simply, the most important *High-Level Creative Function* of all. It's facilitated by your *Genius*, of course, the part of you that gets its information from outside your linear understanding. A true *Vision* is free of your *Compensating Logic* and uninfluenced by what you logically assume to be possible or not. And whether you appreciate it at first or not, because it is formulated by your *Genius*, a true *Vision* can be relied upon to be both possible and a reflection of what you truly care about.

All throughout history, in every culture and civilization, the "vision quest" has been an important theme. The societies of antiquity developed all kinds of systems to encourage and aid their members in realizing their true natures and destinies, which should tell you something about the relevance of such an undertaking when it comes to the actualization of our highest potential. All of the work we do in my *Natural Success* curriculum is ultimately designed to empower participants in being able to make formal *Choices* that reflect their true nature and purpose, and that will inevitably lead to the manifestation of the same.

THE LAND OF PLENTY

To aid their people in formulating a *Geniusly* inspired *Vision* for themselves, many indigenous cultures have a concept of a place one can go to where everything your heart desires already exists. What you find there is what is truly meaningful and important for your spirit to create. The Native Americans call it "the Land of Plenty." Once my students are versed in the mechanics of creating, and trained in *Super Conscious* awareness (so that they may better know themselves and more easily recognize the voice of their own *Genius*) they are introduced to their *Land of Plenty*. I teach them to get there using a very simple yet powerful shamanic technique called the *Blue Mist Exercise*. It's a process that imaginatively transports them to a point in their consciousness where they can access a *Vision* of what they would love to create, free of their *Compensating Logic* and beliefs of separation.

The link below will take you to a recording of the *Blue Mist* visualization, in case you would like to use it to go to your *Land of Plenty* and formulate your own set of *High-Level Creative Choices*. It's a simple little guided meditation. After making your intention to receive the most powerful, *Geniusly* inspired *Vision* possible, you just imagine that you are blue mist floating above the ground. It's important to build a full-sensory experience—really notice what it's like being that mass of swirling blue particles of moisture the whole time. After a minute or two of concentrating on being blue mist, imagine that you're being drawn into a tunnel that goes deep into a mountain. You're blue mist floating down a safe, wide, airy, well-lit tunnel. And just keep noticing what it's like being blue mist floating down a tunnel. Again, after another two minutes, imagine that the tunnel begins ascending at a forty-five-degree angle. Now, as blue mist travelling upwards and forwards through a tunnel, you begin speeding up, and as you speed up you begin turning brighter and brighter blue. Really do your best to imagine that effect. For a minute, imagine that process: going faster and faster; and the faster you go the brighter blue you become, and the brighter you are, the quicker you travel... until you're going so fast you seem to be standing still, and you're so bright you're apparently colorless, transparent even. Really, the only way to achieve a sense of that is to imagine that you can imagine pure emptiness. And it's at this point that you pop out the other side of the tunnel into your *Land of Plenty*. (For an audio of the *Blue Mist Exercise*, please go to williamwhitecloud.com/naturalsuccessbonus/).

Now that you have arrived in your *Land of Plenty*, imagine reforming into your normal human form and you can begin taking stock of what you find there. Remember that this is an intuitive exercise, so what you apprehend in your *Land of Plenty* will be determined by your own intuitive style. You may get a completely visual representation of the full scope of your heart's desire; you may only get a sense of things; it might be a combination of tangible pictures of some things and a more vague sense of other things; or, more unlikely, you may be totally blank. It doesn't matter what's there or not there, because all of the conventions that apply to *Symbol Interpretation* also apply to the *Land of Plenty*. It's up to you to unpack whatever sense you get of your *Vision*. The *Blue Mist* meditation takes you to a purely creative place where you can safely make up what you would truly love to have or go for in life. If you reach the *Land of Plenty* and you're drawing a complete blank, that just means you have permission to make up whatever you fancy. It's important to suspend your reservations about the validity of whatever you find or make up. Let your imagination go and give your desires free reign. You're in an *Ego*-free zone, and no matter what reservations arise, what you conceive in the *Land of Plenty* is sure to have *High-Level Creative* integrity.

Going to the *Land of Plenty* is truly a second chance in life, a chance to be born again into a life orientation that fulfills your true nature and purpose. You owe it to yourself to make a thorough inventory of all that your heart desires. It's an act of self-love to acknowledge your truth. Take your time and have the courage and patience to unearth all the dreams dying to be born, regardless of how little they make sense to you in the moment.

MAKING CHOICES

Caution! If you continue on this path you are about to turn your life upside down and begin the ride of your life. By making *Geniusly inspired Choices*, you are setting a course for yourself that disregards all the conditions you ever believed had to exist for you to be viable in life and embraces whatever it takes for you to live as an expression of your highest potential. From here on, the structures that are inconsistent with you living on a *High-Level Creative Frequency* are going to crumble and the structures that serve your *Genius* life are going to begin establishing themselves. As these new neural pathways, to use a metaphor, begin paving themselves, you will at times experience dismay and alarm. Just remember that the great Sufi poets like Attar and Rumi extolled the virtue of bewilderment, considering it an exalted condition of creativity. The more you hang with the tension of your *Creative Vision*, the more you will come to appreciate what wonders are magically coming together and the less you will care about losing the crutches you used to hobble through life on. It's true that whatever you spent a lifetime figuring out will be rendered meaningless, but now you will be in a sublime mystery, guided by an impeccably *Genius* force, relieved of the responsibility of having to rely on the limitations of your brute strength and the shortsighted calculations of your brain.

Which brings me back to the *Land of Plenty*. Once you have written down or somehow recorded your *Vision* of the things and qualities that fulfill the expression of your highest potential, you then want to extract about eight or nine themes from that inventory. Typically, these can cover anything from a loving, intimate relationship, to your ideal home, to family, vocational fulfillment, artistic expression, travel and adventure, involvement in outreach work, and the passionate pursuit of interests such as sailing, horseback riding, or dancing. You name it, if it's in your *Land of Plenty* it's an end result worthy of your energy. Qualities such as peace of mind, abundance, and zest for life are equally valid. We always want to be sure that we're not reinforcing our preoccupation with conditions we believe need to exist before we can create what we love, but as I've already stressed, if we find it in our *Land of Plenty*, we must assume that it is a legitimate heart desire.

Once you've dissected your *Vision* and extracted the basic themes, your next step is to frame those themes up as formal *Choices*. This means wording them in a way that gives your *Subconscious* a clear message of what you want to manifest in your life. I always suggest that every *Choice* begins with the wording, "I choose the end result of..." Those very words help evoke a connection to the end result of the *Choice*, beyond the process, thereby also evoking the *emotion* of the end result.

As far as the rest of the wording goes, you want the *Choice* to be crisp and clear, saying precisely what you want, but without being too dry and stilted. It's important that when you say the *Choice* to yourself that you can see a picture of what the end result looks like and, very importantly, what it feels like. So, if you have a relationship *Choice*, say, you don't merely word it, "I choose the end result of a great relationship." It's far more preferable to be adding a few juicy adjectives that amplify the qualities of the *Choice*. So, the relationship *Choice* becomes, "I choose the end result of a deeply passionate, intimate, and committed life partnership." Of course, this is not necessarily how you will word your relationship *Choice*; if you have one, yours will be worded according to your sense of what a relationship means and feels like to you.

If you have more than nine themes, which I find rare, to be honest, I strongly recommend that you decide which ones you value most highly, and make sure you ultimately don't have a set of *Foundational Choices* of more than eight or nine. In my own experience, and from observing the creative experience of thousands of other people, loading ourselves up with too many *Choices* dilutes our focus to begin with, and ultimately becomes tiresome and often leads to abandoning the *Choice*-making process altogether. After all, these *Foundational Choices* aren't the only ones you're going to make…

In addition to your *Foundational Choices*, it's very important that you make *Orientational Choices*, too. While your *Foundational Choices* ensure that your energy is consistently focused on what is truly meaningful to you personally, and not driven by what you seek to avoid in life, *Orientational Choices* inform your *Subconscious* of where you fundamentally choose to come from in life. One way of putting it is that they are *Choices* that stand you in your power, fix you to your *High-Level Creative Frequency,* which supports you in going for and manifesting your *Foundational Choices*.

Some examples of *Orientational Choices* are "living as a free spirit" or "creating in line with my highest potential." As far as I'm concerned, there are two *Choices* that between them have it covered: "I choose the end result of living my true nature and purpose" and "I choose the end result of being healthy." No need to load yourself up with excess *Choices* that more or less boil down to the same thing. I believe that if you're living your true nature and purpose, it assumes you are a free spirit manifesting in line with your highest power and potential. Though, equally, I don't believe you can overlook the importance of health. Holding yourself on the razor's edge of your most empowered perspective, and acting in accordance with that truth, takes energy. Developing and maintaining a foundation of physical, mental, and emotional fitness should be something that every creator is dedicated to.

Once you have framed up your *Orientational* and *Foundational Choices*, you have the most essential ingredient for drastically changing your life—and the world, for that matter—for the better. While "the Philosopher's Stone" was in fact an allusion by Alchemists to the transformative power of the imagination, we could be forgiven for believing that the arcane term is a metaphor for *Choices*. They are the pivotal device by which we shift from *Low-Level Creative Function* to *High-Level Creative Function*, thereby transmuting a relatively leaden existence into a golden life.

All that it takes to unleash the power of your *Choices* is to begin making them, of course. By which I mean taking time out every day to say them to yourself—out loud or silently, whichever you prefer. And, importantly, to give each *Choice* juice by imagining yourself in the end result as vividly as you can. It shouldn't take you more than thirty seconds to make each *Choice*, which adds up to a total of six or so minutes for all of your *Orientational* and *Foundational Choices* combined.

This brief daily exercise will be the biggest investment you'll ever make towards living your life as an expression of your highest potential and creating the life you love. Nothing else you do—no amount of studying, working hard, cultivating financial resources, or anything else you can think of—will make as big a difference. That's because the biggest determinant of what creates your reality is the message your *Subconscious* gets about where the power is in your consciousness, and making *Choices* is the process by which you formally assign the power.

I remember catching up with an old friend for coffee one day after not having been in touch for several years. He'd done a lot of work with me in the past, and as a consequence we had a very cordial relationship. I was taken aback, therefore, when, without a hint of malice, he said to me: "Those trainings I did with you were the best days of my life. We had so many peak experiences and laughs. But between you and me, this stuff doesn't work in the real world, does it? I mean, I haven't created a single thing since then."

Once I had recovered from the initial shock of his proposition, I had the presence of mind to establish the most basic fact relevant to continuing the conversation: "Have you been making *Choices* since you completed the trainings?"

"No," my friend answered blithely.

Well, there it was. That explained everything. All of the trainings I run, all of the work I teach, all of the awareness I enable, all of the techniques I impart, are ultimately designed to support people in one thing: making *High-Level Creative Choices*, from which success naturally flows. Of the thousands of people I have trained in *Natural Success*, I'm aware of hundreds who have gone nowhere, and hundreds who have used my model to transform their lives in the most brilliant ways imaginable. I can safely say that there is only one distinction between those who succeed and those who don't—consistent *Choice*-making.

TRUTH, LOVE, AND WISDOM

If I have convinced you to start making *High-Level Creative Choices* then my work here is almost done. Once you begin to make *Super Consciously* derived *Choices*, free of your *Negative Vision*, you're going to *Subconsciously* tap into an inspired level of emotion, which in turn will naturally lead you to a whole new level of insight, effective action, enhanced capability, serendipity, synchronicity, resourcefulness, connections, improved options, and, well, just magic in

Using the Emotion of the True End Result

general. But wait, there's more! Not much more, but definitely some real gold to finish off with.

Whenever I give talks on the themes of either *Natural Success* or *Super Conscious Writing*, I always invite members of the audience to raise their hands if they hate conflict and tension, and if they're interested in learning how to rid themselves of these negative states. A unanimous and enthusiastic show of hands follows. And that's when I tell my audience that, creatively speaking, they are screwed. Their eager smiles are replaced by perplexed frowns.

The fact of the matter is that everything in the universe is created according to the principle of *Tension Seeking Resolution*. I'm not a scientist by any means, but as I understand it, the universe itself was once a tiny, pea-sized ball of energy, which, subject to ever intensifying pressure, exploded in a Big Bang, freeing the energy to expand ever outward, and in the process create galaxies of stars and planets and moons and asteroids, and a multiplicity of life such as exists on Planet Earth. To put it crudely, and speaking of big bangs, you and I are both the product of tension seeking resolution. Nudge, nudge, wink, wink. Whether it is trees in the jungle striving towards sunlight, or single-celled organisms in a test tube retreating from the heat of a Bunsen burner, or air moving from an area of high pressure to an area of low pressure resulting in wind, all end results are the product of tension seeking resolution.

When you seek to eliminate inner tension, you are also unwittingly neutralizing the very energy that can compel the end results you seek to create. What you have to appreciate is that tension doesn't only seek resolution; it always finds a resolution, no matter what. In seeking Fergus Herbert's okay to use his Knights of the Round Table story for this book, Fergus wrote back not only granting permission but also stressing that, for him, the real takeaway was that his fantastic creation was determined by him being able to hang out with the tension all the way through from inception to manifestation.

Alchemists understood this principle very well, and in particular how it applied to consciousness. Their understanding is encapsulated in the Hermetic principle of *Truth, Love, and Wisdom*, which suggests that when you have a *Vision* of where you would love to be (*Love*), and are clear on where you honestly are in relation to that end result (*Truth*), then *Wisdom* will inevitably result. Why, you may ask? Because the discrepancy between where you are and where you want to be sets up a psychic tension that your *Subconscious* is compelled to resolve. It resolves the tension by pushing up *Wisdom* into your *Self Conscious* awareness: you begin making connections between things that haven't been made before—possibilities open up, opportunities suddenly present themselves everywhere. But really, in my experience, it goes further than that. Things begin falling into your lap. Whatever needs to happen for where you are to resemble where you want to be…starts happening. As in Fergus's case, where exactly the perfect business opportunity was dropped in his lap on the last day of his self-imposed deadline.

Truth, Love, and Wisdom

WISDOM

TRUTH   LOVE

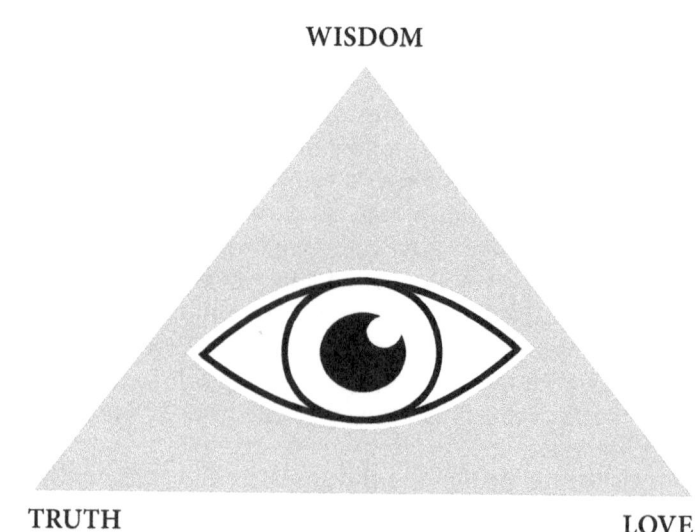

The self-evident example of *Tension Seeking Resolution* in Consciousness is illustrated by the breakthroughs scientists and inventors make in relation to the problems they work on. We hear stories of how their realizations occur to them spontaneously in their downtime, like when they are in the shower or walking the dog. But those inspirations don't just come out of nowhere. They follow periods of the scientist or the inventor being intensely immersed in the problem they face and the solution they seek. Out of sight, their *Subconscious* has been working feverishly on the answer, prompted by the *Creative Tension* it has been subject to.

Rollo May, the highly regarded humanistic psychologist, in his book *The Courage to Create*, postulated that the efficacy of the Oracle at Delphi lay not in any external oracle's psychic power, but within the psyche of the person seeking divination. As they trekked from all over Greece to the shrine of Apollo, pilgrims focused intently every step of the way on their situation and the ideal outcome they wished for. The tension created by the disparity between their *Current Reality* and their *Vision* induced the answer they were seeking. Hence, says May, the inscription above the entrance of the temple, "*Know thyself.*"

Proper contemplation of this principle will highlight the weakness in our conditioned tendency to avoid tension, as well as the limitation of concepts that deny either *Vision* or *Current Reality*. I shudder to think of the false wisdom exemplified in the statement, "Don't be attached to the outcome." Equally, I shake my head despairingly at the mindless adherence to "manifesting" techniques such as *Positive Thinking* and *Positive Affirmations*. Having a positive outlook in life is definitely a desirable attitude, but that outlook becomes self-defeating, and even destructive, when it is divorced from reality. And affirming an end result is a creatively positive action, though all too often people who use affirmations say them motivated by their sense of lack, and also in willful denial of the *Truth* of where they currently are.

The empowered creator is so because they don't see *Current Reality* as a negative condition that precludes anything from turning out the way they would love it to be. They define inner conflict as a potent tool for self-awareness, and the *Truth* that arises from objective awareness—no matter how pleasant or unpleasant—as one of the ingredients that gives rise to the *Subconscious* tension that puts them on a *High-Level Creative Frequency* and compels the end results of their choosing. If you mean to develop the power to create your life as a work of art and magic, then you too should get excited about the transformative potential of your *Current Reality*, regardless of how favorable or unfavorable you ever judge it to be.

Given the idea of *Creative Tension*, you won't be surprised, then, that when it comes to making *Choices*, I advocate you not only make the *Choices* as I have prescribed, which is to visualize the end result and repeat the wording of each *Choice*, but that you also establish the *Current Reality* relating to each of them. Though, let me hasten to add that it isn't necessary to look at the *Current Reality* of every *Choice* every day. You never want *Choice*-making to be a big chore. It is enough to take two different *Choices* a day and look at the *Truth* of where you are relative to the ideal of where you would *Love* to be. If you do the math, you will see that you are covering the *Current Reality* of each of your *Choices* at least once a week, which is plenty. First off, much of the *Current Reality* of any given *Choice* will relate to several of your other *Choices*, something you will notice once you begin making them. Secondly, by acknowledging the *Current Reality* of those two *Choices* you are, in a way, reminding your *Subconscious* of the divide that exists in all of your *Choices* between where you actually are and your desired destination.

You don't need to spend more than thirty seconds per *Choice* on *Current Reality* if you look at it intuitively. By going into *In No Sense* and allowing yourself to receive a sense of where you are, you will quickly get a picture of your position, both in terms of logical, practical factors and, very importantly, psychological factors (don't forget, the second step of *Natural Success* is hearing what your *Unconscious* is telling you). If, as an example, we suppose you are choosing to buy a flashy new motor vehicle, what may occur to you is the reality of your financial situation and, maybe, that such a luxury item is inconsistent with your sense of worth, or lack thereof.

So, you can see, including the *Current Reality* of two *Choices* a day should only add a minute to your *Choice*-making practice. And yet, by doing so, you set up a groove in your consciousness that can only flow to your inevitably manifesting what you would love to create in life, and your living your life as an expression of your highest potential. The *Creative Tension* you establish by holding *Love* and *Truth* simultaneously will transport you to a level of creative power you never dreamed of. One of the most important benefits of *Creative Tension*, aside from those already enumerated, is that you will naturally be more inclined to take action and follow through on the *Wisdom* that arises as a product of making *Choices*. Not only will you have a heightened sense of knowing, but also a greater compulsion to follow through on your knowing, to do what obviously needs to be done. All you have to do to set up this magical groove is contemplate your *Vision* for no more than thirty seconds, contemplate your current circumstances for no more than thirty seconds, and then put the power in the *Vision* by choosing it.

CREATIVE TENSION VS. STRESS

Of course, it would be misleading, and an insult to most people's intelligence, to suggest that manifesting what you want is as simple as *Vision*, *Current Reality*, and *Choice*. Setting up your magical groove is that simple, but holding yourself in that groove is another matter. As Plato so keenly observed, "There exists in the Universe a blind refractory force which denies the will of God."

When you study filmmaking, one of the most important aspects of storytelling that you learn is that the opponent, or baddie, is always more powerful than the hero. If you see a Bond film, for instance, the villain's strongman usually beats James Bond in their first fight at the beginning of the movie. This obviously sets up the suspense for the final battle scene, where you, the audience, anxiously wait to see how the hero will overcome the opponent to achieve their result of saving the day, or in Bond's case, the world. You will notice that the baddie can't be defeated by brute force alone. To win, the hero has to dig deep within and draw on an inner creative resource, like cunning or quick-wittedness.

This mythological dynamic reflects a profound psychological truth. Your *Ego* is always stronger than your *Self Conscious* will. Let me explain. The *Ego* is your vehicle of orientation and, as such, when you make a *Choice* to go for something, your *Ego* wants to figure out how to get there. The problem is that the *Ego* doesn't look at the factors objectively relevant to the situation or the functional steps required. Instead, it refers to your *Unconscious Belief System*, determines what it believes is incomplete about you, and then proposes resolving your sense of incompleteness as the first order of business. Your *Ego* communicates its sense of incompleteness to you through emotional discomfort such as shame, guilt, anger, fear, inadequacy, confusion, doubt, boredom, emptiness, and so on. Resolving that *Emotional Tension* becomes the name of the game. Now, suddenly, you have *Emotional Tension* competing with *Creative Tension*.

Trying to force your way through *Emotional Tension* is futile. Believe me, the *Ego* is not interested in you getting what you love. Its sole concern is survival, which it assumes depends on you fixing yourself and remedying your inadequacies. So, when you stay focused on your end result in spite of any inner conflict, your *Ego* just ramps up the *Emotional Tension* to the level required for you to pay exclusive attention to its priorities. Now you experience your *Emotional Tension* as stress, and stress will kill your focus on the end result, and thereby your *Creative Tension*, every time. Unless you're initiated in the dynamics of creating, the only way to mitigate the *Ego's* response to *Creative Tension*—stress—is to cut down on or give up on your *Vision*, or to abandon seeing your *Current Reality*, or both. This will inevitably happen. *Emotional Tension*, elevated to the level of stress, will grind down *Creative Tension* every time.

An informed insight into the competing forces of *Creative Tension* and *Emotional Tension* helps us see through the misconceptions of many spiritual and creative models that exist in the world today. Generally—and let me repeat, generally—Eastern modalities advocate *being* over *doing* and are averse to wanting things, because desire, as they see it, creates suffering. Western modalities are the opposite, in that they tend to advocate relentless striving facilitated by the willful denial of practical circumstances and emotional realities. While the former promotes a passive acceptance of the status quo in return for an absence of inner conflict, the latter regards the sacrifice of truth and inner harmony as acceptable casualties of achievement and material reward. It's as if the one way prefers to deny that we humans have a heart, that there are things that are deeply important for us to have, that we are endowed with a higher potential that seeks expression; and that the other way does indulge our creative urge, but believes that in order for us to create we have to lock our hearts in a steel safe and throw away the key. Neither orientation honors our full creative capacity or demonstrates a complete grasp of the natural principles of creativity. As such, they fall well short of tapping our full potential, and quite evidently don't do much by way of the fulfillment of our *Creative Spirit*.

But the Hermetic philosophers knew better. They taught that nothing creative is achieved by way of presumptuous denial; that, in fact, masterful manifesting is a function of using law against law. One law—or premise, as we prefer—of consciousness is that your *Ego* is activated every time you contemplate or decide on going for something. It's actually not a malicious force; it really wants to help you understand how to get what you want. The only problem is that its involvement in the process leads to *Emotional Tension*, which, if ignored, will turn into stress, which in turn will kill your will to hold *Creative Tension*. And yet, if we have a complete understanding of the laws of consciousness, we can overcome stress without compromising our allegiance to seeing our *Current Reality* and going for our *Vision*.

For a start, we need to keep in mind the second step of *Natural Success*: hearing what your *Unconscious* is telling you. As long as you're unaware of the messages implicit in your charged emotions, you're going to be subject to them. You'll have no choice other than to resolve them by worrying and acting out according to their dictates, thereby giving them even more power. Meanwhile, all they really want is for you to hear them out. By you becoming conscious of what your uncomfortable feelings are telling you, they don't need to call out louder and louder for your attention. Even more to the point, when you appreciate the rubbish they're telling you, you won't be able to take them seriously. Your *Self Conscious* discernment gets passed on to your *Subconscious*, which then also takes your *Unconscious* messages less seriously. Right away you will notice your *Emotional Tension* dissipating.

Next, we can use what we learned in the third step of *Natural Success*. Because the *Ego* is our vehicle of orientation, it is engaged when our attention is overly focused on understanding how we are going to create our desired end result. Any time you are emotionally agitated or stressed, and you take a moment to notice what's going on for you, you will quickly realize that you are busy trying to rationally work out your situation, whether that's a dilemma you find yourself in or an outcome you're working towards.

In the creative orientation, where we approach life from our *High-Level Creative Frequency*, we don't operate by working things out. We rely on being guided by our *Super Conscious* intuition, which gets through to us when we relax our need to understand. The state of *In No Sense* has a two-fold benefit: it calms our emotions and empowers us with a functional awareness of where we are and what we can practically do about it. Once we make a *Choice*, it is vital that we keep letting go of the "how." After all, *Creative Tension* is going to provide us with all the *Wisdom* we need in relation to manifesting the *Choice*. Quite frankly, if you can't let go of the need to understand and work everything out, you're doomed to being limited to what you know and learned to expect from the past—and catching a bad case of emotional dis-ease.

And finally, the pièce de résistance! Transmuting *Emotional Tension* into *Creative Tension*. Having the power to minimize our stress levels is most certainly both a relief and a creative advantage. The real game-changer, though, is the realization that *Emotional Tension* can actually be transformed into *Creative Tension*. Whenever you make a *Choice* by establishing the *Vision*, acknowledging *Current Reality*, and assigning the power by choosing the *Vision* over your circumstances, you are instituting *Creative Tension*. But at the same time you are also unwittingly instigating a competing dynamic, namely *Emotional Tension*. Unless *Emotional Tension* is squarely addressed, it will have a tendency to get nasty.

As you have seen, two ways of keeping *Emotional Tension* in check are being with your painful feelings and hearing them out, and letting go of the "how." But even more powerful than these two strategies put together is incorporating your *Emotional Tension* into *Creative Tension* by including it as part of your *Current Reality*. If you think about it, all at once this acknowledges your emotional reality, establishes *Creative Tension* at a deeper level, and assigns the power to the desired end result or *Vision* over the *Current Reality*, in which *Emotional Tension* is now nested. When this technique becomes part of a consistent creative practice, your *Subconscious* will begin feeding predominantly off the emotion of your desired end results, and you will begin to experience powerful results in your life, as well as a much more uplifted emotional experience along with it. You will truly begin to appreciate how awesome it is to live life on a *High-Level Creative Frequency*.

Emotional Tension Incorporated In Creative Tension

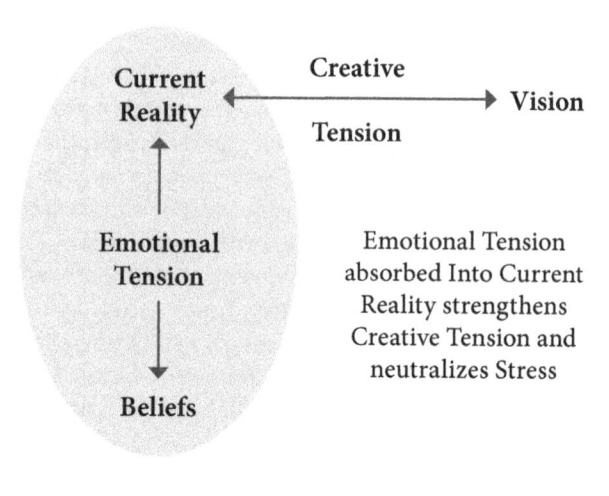

```
         Creative
Current ←----------→ Vision
Reality    Tension

   ↑
Emotional    Emotional Tension
Tension      absorbed Into Current
   ↓         Reality strengthens
             Creative Tension and
Beliefs      neutralizes Stress
```

TWENTY MINUTES THAT CAN CHANGE YOUR LIFE FOR GOOD

It is fitting that I finished writing this manuscript on a recent visit to Australia. While I was Down Under, I had the opportunity of meeting with many past *Natural Success* graduates, and learning about what they have done with their lives in the time I have been living in California. I won't lie to you, half of them have gone nowhere, and their lives tell the familiar tale of human struggle and suffering. The other half, though, have created not just brilliant lives for themselves, but if you knew the horrific circumstances some started out from, you would agree that the term *miraculous* is totally justified when applied to their stories. I asked every one of the grads I spent time with whether they made

Choices. The battlers answered "Never," or "Hardly ever," and every single person whose life is on the up and up looked me straight in the eye and said, "Every day."

Perhaps the most delightful reunion was with my good friends Karen and Peter Hutton. We caught up at The Italian, a swank eatery in my old hometown of Byron Bay, owned by another friend, genius restaurateur Laurie Rose. You won't meet a more stylish, gracious, warm, or witty couple than Karen and Peter. They are simply the best. It was wonderful to share a few bottles of rosé and plates of Pacific oysters with them, as the sun sank into a red haze behind our backs and flocks of rainbow lorikeets noisily claimed the towering Norfolk pines around us as their roosts. More than anything, it was so uplifting to hear how well they and their young adult kids were doing as a loving, cohesive family, what a huge success the couple had made of their business, and what a great lifestyle they were living, regularly travelling to exotic overseas destinations and splitting their time equally between the city of Brisbane and laid-back Byron Bay. Their account was all the more inspiring considering that it wasn't always the latest-model Mercedes Benzes, Rolex watches, and luxury safaris in India for the Huttons. In fact, it was quite the opposite some years back.

Theirs is not a rags to riches story, though. Peter had been a very successful realtor, and even recognized with an international award for his outstanding work in real estate. But at some point his passion for his business died. He sold his agency and retired to Byron Bay, where he hoped he would find himself, along with a new direction in life.

Those were some fun times—for a while, anyway. Days were spent lazing on white-sand beaches and painting very respectable impressionist artworks. Nights were a seamless bohemian soirée, with a flow of good wine, and music and laughter floating from Casa Hutton all the way down the street. I know I spent many an evening at their beachside bungalow, mesmerized by the enchanted spell of flawless hospitality. But, like the Byron Bay beaches, where dangerous undercurrents belie the seemingly benign beauty of the ocean, stressful forces were beginning to run counter to the joie de vivre we, their friends, witnessed on the surface.

The Huttons were running out of money and Peter wasn't having any luck coming up with anything satisfying that he could do to make money. In the end, he decided to go back into business as a consultant providing sales and marketing training to real estate agents. I had no judgment of whether it was a *Negative Vision* or not; it seemed like a good fit. Peter had a proven track record in that business sector and from my experience of him, he certainly cared about people being empowered to be the best they could be. I expected nothing from Peter other than a smooth road back to a purposeful and profitable career.

It wasn't to be, though. I lost contact with the Huttons, pretty much, when they left Byron Bay and moved back to Brisbane. I was only hearing second- or third-hand reports that Peter was having a very rough time establishing himself as a player in his field. There was even a rumor that he had been forced to declare himself bankrupt. All the bad news was confirmed one day when Peter called me and asked for my help. Could I provide any insight into why he was struggling in spite of his great talents, depth of experience, hard work, and the seemingly ripe pickings to be had in the real estate consultancy business? Considering he was a graduate of my courses, and all the good friendship he had shown me, I naturally had no hesitation in obliging.

I suggested we use the trusty old *Conflict Deconstruction Exercise* to investigate the structural causes of Peter's difficulties. In about two minutes we had established that *Unconsciously* Peter defined the world as some sort of club that others belonged to and he did not. Deep down, below his *Self Conscious* awareness, he perceived that he was inherently blackballed from the exclusive coterie of established real estate consultants. When I asked him to connect with the pain of not belonging and then tell me what that wounded emotion was urging him to do, I could already hear the pennies dropping for Peter as he replied, "The feeling is telling me to compete aggressively with the people in the

Using the Emotion of the True End Result

club, to undermine their methods, and show them up as second-rate."

"So, what has your relationship with your competition been?" I asked, already sure of what the answer would be.

"I've been taking a lot of shots at them," said my friend hesitantly. I could picture him nodding thoughtfully at the other end of the line.

"So, notice how your energy is going into your perceived barrier to entry into the consultancy space," I pointed out. "How's that working for you?"

I didn't have to spell it out for Peter. He could take it from there. "I'm creating a massive barrier for myself. The opposition is totally united in pushing back and challenging my credibility. Geez! No wonder I'm struggling to attract an audience. There isn't much goodwill for me out there in the market."

From there, I asked Peter to put aside the problem for a moment and answer a completely independent question. What would he love? After some time he came back with a considered reply. He would love to empower real estate salespeople to achieve fantastic results through reliance on their innate integrity, passion, and creativity.

"So, if you feel into the emotion of that end result, what is that emotion urging you to do, or how is it compelling you to be?" I quizzed Peter.

"To get over myself and serve the industry, not myself, with good cheer and goodwill." A shiver of delight ran down my back. That sounded exactly like the friend I knew talking.

After discussing the insights gained from the exercise, I asked Peter what his essential takeaway was. Again, he was thoughtful in his reply. "I never realized how much energy I was putting into maligning my peers, or even that I was doing it. And just how much it's my own actions that are causing me to be shut out of the real estate consultants club. I just need to go back to focusing on my true end result and do what I do with love and respect."

Our conversation took only about twenty minutes but I know it played a major part in turning the Huttons' fortunes around. What I saw from that point on was that Peter took his attention off what the other consultants were doing and put his energy into being the great marketer and salesman he was wanting to empower others to be. Amazingly (though unsurprisingly, because I really believe that there isn't such a thing as competition), the hotshot consultants in his space didn't only let up on their denouncements of him, they actually began to cooperate with him and help him become a fully fledged member of their club.

As a result of his highly creative approach, along with allowing himself to receive the support of his peers, Peter did succeed in becoming a well-established, top-notch consultant in the real estate field. So much so that he was recruited as a highly paid in-house trainer for one of the most prestigious real estate franchises in the country. He relished being back in the business so much that the owner of an estate agency eventually succeeded in persuading him to get back into the game practicing what he preached. Of course, powering on his *High-Level Creative Frequency* as he now was, Peter was never going to last long working for someone else. Ultimately, he and Karen opened the upmarket real estate firm Hutton and Hutton, where both of them work to this day.

What is especially wonderful to behold is how effortlessly the Huttons create their success and lifestyle. Peter still pursues his passion for painting while Karen indulges her love of fashion and interior design. Along with their travels and nearly half the week spent chilling in Byron Bay, it's almost as if they incidentally run a thriving multimillion-dollar real estate business on the side. But don't be fooled. Their success is born of a canny foreknowledge of the emerging trends in their industry and their boldly capitalizing on that wisdom. And that *Genius* edge is born of Karen and Peter having a very fierce *Vision* of what they are creating. Which isn't a supposition on my part, by the way; they told me as much over dinner.

Really, the Huttons are the urban version of the African scout I wrote about in the story of the albino wildebeest at the beginning of the book. They embody the truth that we live in a benign universe ever guiding us to the most optimum experience of life possible, and that if we can devote ourselves to developing the ability to hear and follow that guidance, then the fruits of *Natural Success* will be ours to enjoy. That ability is inside all of us, not just that native tracker, or Steve Jobs, or J.K. Rowling, or Wag Dodge, or Musashi, or Casanova, or Harriet Tubman, or the Huttons.

Knowing in your heart—and mind—that this is true, may you enjoy the boundless success of a fully wise Alchemist.

ABOUT THE AUTHOR

William Whitecloud's connection to the magical nature of life can be traced back to his childhood in the small African country of Eswatini, where he was immersed in the super-natural worldview of the tribes people around him.

This association was reinforced when he immigrated to Australia in 1983 and began speculating on global financial money markets, using profoundly esoteric methods for predicting market movements. Over time William's attention shifted from observing phenomena at work outside of himself to finding ways he could practically apply magic to creating what truly mattered to him in his own life. This search brought him into contact with the alchemical principles of Hermetic Philosophy and the ideas of Robert Fritz, founder of Technologies For Creating.

Within months, he had begun to study and teach these superbly effective modalities for reconnecting with and manifesting what is truly important to the human spirit. William went on to found his own Natural Success modality, dedicated to empowering participants in discovering and living their authentic nature and purpose. Through his involvement in the program, he has worked with thousands of individuals, training and coaching them in bringing their dreams into reality. His ongoing search to discern the essence of what it takes people to connect with and live from their creative spirit forms the basis of his books, The Magician's Way and The Last Shaman.

William now lives in California where he devotes his time to coaching, writing, making films, enjoying his family, and letting life unfold by magic.

Follow and connect with William

www.williamwhitecloud.com

https://www.instagram.com/williamwhitecloud/

https://twitter.com/willwhitecloud

https://www.facebook.com/williamwhitecloud

Other titles by William

THE MAGICIAN'S WAY

THE LAST SHAMAN

Notes

Notes

Notes